A Feminist Theory of Violence

"In this robust, decolonial challenge to carceral feminism, Françoise Vergès elucidates why a structural approach to violence is needed. If we wish to understand how racial capitalism is linked to the proliferation of intimate and state violence directed at women and gender-nonconforming people, we need to look no further than Vergès' timely analysis."

Angela Y. Davis, Distinguished Professor Emerita,
University of California, Santa Cruz

"A powerful and uncompromising text … A stunning reflection on the recurrence of assault—gender-based, sexual, racial violence."

Terrafemina

"An important and courageous book, which raises difficult questions and uncovers invisible structures of domination."

Trou Noir

"Vergès' incandescent writing casts a light on the global inequalities, brutal carceral systems, unfettered militarization, and punitive ideologies that shape violent intimacies."

Laleh Khalili, Professor of International Politics,
Queen Mary University of London

"A call to join in the urgent decolonial feminist work of rethinking the practices of (so-called) protection outside of the logics of violence. We have the ability, Vergès insists, to enact a post violent society, to bring another world into being."

Christina Sharpe, Canada Research Chair in Black Studies in the Humanities, York University, Toronto and author of *In the Wake: On Blackness and Being*

"A road map of radical emancipatory imaginaries for shaping urgent social and political change. Vergès' arguments rise from the ground up, from the lived experience of grassroots dissent, action and mobilization against the wounds and damages inflicted by extractive capitalism across the world."

Rasha Salti, curator of art and film

Also available by Françoise Vergès:

A Decolonial Feminism

"A vibrant and compelling framework for feminism in our times."
Judith Butler

"A powerful tool of social transformation."
Djamila Ribeiro, Brazilian human rights activist

"Incisive … an invitation to reconnect with the utopian
power of feminism."
Aurelien Maignant, *Fabula*

'A powerful work.'
Les Inrocks

"Develops a critical perspective on feminism to reconsider the
conditions of possibility and purpose … resituates feminism in
a truly political, emancipatory and critical dimension."
Jean-Philippe Cazier, *Diacritik*

"Essential for highlighting the current divisions within feminist
political agendas, and for collective reflection on a profound,
radical transformation of society … Necessary reading."
Axelle n°219

A Feminist Theory of Violence

A Decolonial Perspective

Françoise Vergès

Translated by Melissa Thackway

First published 2020 as *Une Théorie féministe de la violence* by La Fabrique Éditions
English language edition first published 2022 by Pluto Press
New Wing, Somerset House, Strand, London WC2R 1LA
www.plutobooks.com

Cet ouvrage a bénéficié du soutien du Programme d'aide à la publication de
l'Institut français

INSTITUT
FRANÇAIS

This book has been selected to receive financial assistance from English PEN's
PEN Translates programme, supported by Arts Council England. English PEN
exists to promote literature and our understanding of it, to uphold writers'
freedoms around the world, to campaign against the persecution and imprisonment
of writers for stating their views, and to promote the friendly co-operation of
writers and the free exchange of ideas. www.englishpen.org

Supported using public funding by
**ARTS COUNCIL
ENGLAND**

British Library Cataloguing in Publication Data
A catalogue record for this book is available from the British Library

ISBN	978 0 7453 4568 0	Hardback
ISBN	978 0 7453 4567 3	Paperback
ISBN	978 0 7453 4571 0	PDF
ISBN	978 0 7453 4569 7	EPUB

This book is printed on paper suitable for recycling and made from fully managed
and sustained forest sources. Logging, pulping and manufacturing processes are
expected to conform to the environmental standards of the country of origin.

Typeset by Stanford DTP Services, Northampton, England

Simultaneously printed in the United Kingdom and United States of America

Contents

Preface to the English Edition

Reports about all forms of violence are so numerous every day, that the feeling that what I wrote a year ago is already obsolete has been haunting. Yet, that feeling should be resisted. What I wrote in 2020 on structural and systemic violence still stands: neoliberal capitalism, racism, imperialism, white supremacy and patriarchy, homophobia and transphobia, are showing their insatiable appetite for domination and oppression. The Western way of life, adopted now also by elites in the Global South, rests on the normalization of violence, on making violence not only inevitable but also necessary. Images of what is shown as the *good* life abound in glossy magazines, in films, or in TV series—clean neighborhoods, houses with luxurious gardens, healthy children laughing while playing on clean beaches, women doing yoga in serene landscapes, hipsters with trimmed beards that do not get them racially profiled, vacations in beautiful places from which the poor are evicted, white saviors doing good deeds, electric cars to save the planet, leisure that cultivates one's mind, food that is grown with respect to the planet... They construct a visual world that adheres to a beauty and harmony which masks its attending violence. Its protection is then presented as the fight of civilization against barbarism, plagues, violence, gangs, violence against women and girls. Protection is understood in the colonial tradition: keep the barbarians at the gates; militarize the public space; create social, environmental, and cultural segregation; use artwashing, politics of bourgeois respect-ability and white feminism to justify this segregation. The wealth that has allowed this good life was accumulated thanks to the extraction of cheap energy (coal and hydrocarbons), the looting and plundering of natural resources by colonial powers. The well-being of European and North American populations was built at the expense of the colonized world. This good life, that reveals a constant stark inequality between North and South, rests on the super-exploitation of the Global South's resources, on the exhaustion, until premature death, of the life force and energy of Black and brown peoples. That it must be protected by all means is taken for granted, for is it not the sign of progress and civilization, and the object of envy and desire by "the rest"?

Violence is consubstantial to racial capitalism; it is not something that comes afterwards, the act of some extreme groups. Ecosystem degradation is accelerated by capitalism, which intensifies pollution and waste, deforestation, land-use change and exploitation, and carbon-driven energy systems. Rape, land theft, genocide, massacres, assassinations, destruction of public services, processes of enslavement, creation of private militias, torture, censorship, have always been the tools of colonialism and capitalism disguised as civilizing missions or humanitarian interventions. Imperialist wars leave behind ruins, pollution, devastation and misery and their "end" means that war is pursued through other means. Afghanistan, Palestine, Iraq, are the current names of this kind of war.

Rage and anger against this destructive machine are justified and legitimate, they open the way to an anti-racist decolonial feminist politics of protection. It is a politics that rejects all the pacifying strategies that barely hide the fact that racism is the organizing principle of carceral feminism, of the idea that women cannot be mobilized to commit acts of violence associated with maleness, of the plantation regime, the civilizing mission, and of corporate philanthropy.

This is why this book takes the point of view that there is an equal opportunity to perpetuate violence and racism, that the offer to exercise domination is made to all, but also that protection cannot be left to those who have divided others' lives between those who deserve protection and those who do not, between those who will live because they accept the rules dictated by the white savior and those who can be abandoned, maimed, killed.

Those who produce a sense of belonging to communities in struggle, who experience the onslaught of racial capitalism and yet, every day, everywhere in the world, who are standing up, are writing, singing, striking, occupying cities, universities, museums, factories, who are pulling down statues that are the symbols of slavery, racism, fascism, and imperialism, who are organizing communal kitchens, who are organizing refuges and sanctuaries for those fleeing wars, climate catastrophes, poverty, and all forms of oppression, those who chose revolutionary love, revolutionary peace over the politics of murder and destruction, are those who are activating and imagining an anti-racist politics of protection. They nurture hope which opens up a possibility of change. Their actions affirm that, yes, it is possible to build a post-capitalist, post-racist, post-patriarchal world. They put into practice an anti-racist politics of protection.

Françoise Vergès
October 2021

To write is to owe a debt, a debt to all the authors of books, poems, novels, films, art installations, and to the activists who have explored, analyzed, and theorized class, race, and gender-based, colonial, imperialist, capitalist, sexist, and sexual oppression. I hereby acknowledge my debt: it is immense.

Introduction

"The oppressive State is a macho rapist."[1]

"The rapist is you. / It's the cops, the judges, the State, the President. / Patriarchy is a judge that imprisons us at birth. / And our punishment is this violence you now see. / It's femicide, impunity for my killer. / It's disappearances. / It's rape. / And it's not my fault, nor where I was, nor what I wore. / The rapist was you. / The rapist is you. / It's the cops, the judges, the State, the President. / The oppressive State is a macho rapist."[2] These are the words of the militant performance that soon went viral around the world, *Un violador en tu camino* ("A Rapist in Your Path"). The text's authors, Dafne Valdés, Paula Cometa, Sibila Sotomayor, and Lea Cáceres—four of the founders of the Chilean feminist collective Las Tesis—pointed the finger at those truly responsible for femicide and rape: the police and the State. Chanted by a collective taking part in the demonstrations against the country's neoliberal policies, chanted in a context of extreme police violence, this song marked a refusal to break ranks with the movement in the name of women's protection: "We categorically refuse to say that the Chilean police ensure women's safety. That is why we are accusing them: to reveal the contradiction, the irony", they declared in the newspaper *Verne*.[3] As the philosopher Elsa Dorlin argues, given that the State is the "principal instigator of inequalities," and considering that it is "precisely the one who arms those who beat us," there is "no point appealing to it for justice because it is precisely the first instance that institutionalizes social injustice."[4] This being so, the fight against violence cannot eschew a critique of the women whom the State promotes and legitimizes, nor of feminist appeals to the State and to the justice system. How to respond to this multifaceted sexist and sexual violence when "racialized bodies, female bodies, poor bodies, or young bodies have less value in this phase of necro-liberal reactivation,"[5] when they are sacrificeable?

As the instance that regulates economic and political domination, the State condenses all forms of imperialist, patriarchal, and capitalist oppression and exploitation. The State as an institution is thus far from playing a small part in the organization and perpetuation of violence against women, poor, and racialized people. In recent years, the neoconservative and neoliberal patriarchy incarnated by various State leaders (Donald Trump, Jair Bolsonaro, Matteo Salvini, to name but a few) has imposed drastic setbacks on women's rights in both their private and professional worlds. It has fomented and encouraged hatred against minorities, trans people, queer people, sex workers, racialized people, migrants, and Muslims. This patriarchal revival is inextricably linked to neoliberal capitalism; it constantly undermines hard-won social rights; it "uberizes" and makes people's existences more precarious. This economy itself generates its own array of discreet yet no less real forms of violence: the exhaustion of bodies, of the oceans, and the earth in the quest for profit, the drastic reduction of life expectancy for the most vulnerable. This patriarchal and neoconservative turn is all the more violent as it more often than not depends on a racial capitalism that is precisely characterized by the premature death of non-white people, as Ruth Wilson Gilmore demonstrates. For racism, she writes, is "the state-sanctioned or extra legal production and exploitation of group-differentiated vulnerability to premature death."[6] In other words, women and men die younger because of racism, which, from birth, fragilizes their access to health and isolates them in jobs that more rapidly exhaust their bodies. Racism, which, as Stuart Hall pointed out, traverses class relations, is thus a central factor in the analysis of the systemic violence that causes highly differentiated death rates according to social and racial belonging.

A decolonial feminism cannot conceivably separate "violence against women" or against "minorities" from a global state of violence: the children who commit suicide in refugee camps, the police and military's massive recourse to rape in armed conflict, systemic racism, the exile of millions of people due to the multiplication of war zones and to economic and climatic conditions that have rendered zones of living uninhabitable, femicide, and the relentless increase in precarity. Can we imagine addressing only part of this violence without considering the rest? Can we continue to feign not to see that all of these forms of violence mutually reinforce one another, and that those which more directly affect women are the result of an extremely violent society? The recent mobilization against gender-based and sexual violence offers a theoretical and practical opportunity: that of making this violence the very terrain on which to challenge patriarchal capitalism.

In this book, I avoid viewing patriarchy through the female victim / male perpetrator prism—even if there are many among the latter who uncontestably deserve this qualification. I propose a critique of dependency on the police and the judicialization of social issues—in other words, of the spontaneous recourse to the criminal justice system to protect so-called "vulnerable" populations. My analysis does not offer solutions for the eradication of gender-based and sexual violence—whose denunciation today reveals its incredible prevalence—but aims to contribute to the reflection on violence as a structural element of patriarchy and capitalism, rather than specifically male. This book attempts to imagine a

4

post-violent society—not a society without conflicts or contradictions, but a society that does not naturalize violence, that does not celebrate it, that does not make it the central theme of its narrative of power. It seeks to answer the following questions: how to deracialize and depatriarchalize the politics of protection? Why has protecting girls and women become an argument that reinforces the police and the justice system's field of action? What is the rationale of carceral feminism? How to explain the proliferation of measures and laws protecting women when women from the working classes and racialized communities face increasing precarity? Why, in a context of the rapid militarization of public space, do feminists aspire to giving greater power to (racist) police?

These questions raise others. Who are these women that the patriarchal State considers worthy of protection? How to explain the State's differentiation of children who have the right to a protected childhood and those who do not? What is the State's role in the reproduction of violence against women? What constitutes a decolonial feminist politics destined to make fear "change sides"? Must protection depend on repression? To access spaces where we can circulate freely, must we increase militarized protection measures: walls, borders, surveillance, extra police powers, and the increased right to use armed force?

A decolonial feminist politics of protection

All societies organize forms of protection for newborn babies, children, the sick, the elderly, and so on. The State has gradually been entrusted with organizing institutions of protection. Other works have highlighted the limits of this model and proposed alternative forms of protection of childhood, the sick, the elderly, female workers, and nature. State control of protection, its bureaucratization, its militarization, and the marginalization, or even erasure, of community-based practices are not directly the object of this book. The aim here, rather, is to imagine forms of protection that do not involve repression, surveillance, prison, and developmentalist paternalism. It might immediately be objected in response to this proposal that, even by dismantling the racialized structure of society and capitalism, violence against women would not be entirely eradicated because it is not exclusively produced by these structures. That is true of course, but it cannot be overstated how much colonialism and capitalism have contributed to the emergence and perpetuation of patriarchy. During colonization, the patriarchy was racialized; a man could be a tyrant at home yet nothing but a Black, Arab, or Asian in the public space—in other words, he could not entirely claim the name of "man." Colonial laws criminalized homosexuality, non-binary gender identities, and family structures that did not conform to the norms of the white bourgeois patriarchal family, and they separated children from their families to "civilize" them. Colonialism racialized sexualities and gender, and imposed male and female beauty norms. Today, these representations and practices remain. In France, during the major postcolonial migrations of the second half of the twentieth century, they contributed to defining family migration policies and the place of women in them. In what is known as the "French Overseas Territories"—territories of colonial empire, slavery, and post-slavery that still come under French rule—they justified babies and children being torn away from their families to be sent to France (the case of the 2,500 Réunionese children sent to rural *départements* of France, known as the "Creuse children"). They also shaped French-style Islamophobia, the stigmatization and discrimination of women who wear the hijab, the criminalization of Black and Arab youth, and de facto (if not *de jure*) instigated a license to kill Black and Arab men.

Imagining a politics of protection based on decolonial and anti-racist feminist analyses implies recognizing the need to protect human beings (babies, children, the elderly, people in situations of vulnerability) without turning them into victims, and without considering weakness as a failing.

In neoliberalism, the efficient body is that of a white man in full possession of physical strength normalized as masculine, who gets up early, goes jogging, eats organic food, and, without counting his hours, works to achieve economic success. What this representation of the able-bodied hides is that its efficiency is made possible by the work of racialized bodies—the women who cleaned his gym, his office, the restaurant he fixes his appointments in, the hotel where he hangs out with his friends, lovers, or sex workers, the train or plane he takes, the classroom he teaches in, the house where he goes home to his family—all these women who are invisibilized and whose bodies are exhausted so that his can excel. Racialized men are his world's security guards; the people of the Global South provide him and his family with the objects of their comfort. The able-bodied is protected by a whole host of police measures, which are invisibilized too, for they are naturalized, guaranteeing its protection: gated communities, surveillance cameras, increased police presence, and so forth. As for the white bourgeoise woman, she more often than not buys her comfort thanks to the exploitation of young women and girls in the Global South: the fast-fashion clothes that enable her to keep up with the latest trends, her children's nanny, the cleaning women who clean the world she moves in, the exploited nurses, the sex workers who cater to her husband. Shut away in their enclaves, the able-bodied exclude bodies perceived as threatening, who only enter their world under authorization, or with a pass, at risk of being arrested for no reason, and in complete impunity.

A decolonial and anti-racist politics of protection is resolutely anti-capitalist and de-patriarchal as it considers these
regimes to be the crucible of systemic violence against women.
It seeks to imagine what a politics of peacefulness might be; to
understand why peace does not designate a durable state, but
rather a simple respite between two armed conflicts; why war
is so easily seen to be the response to any conflict, or even
as the only way to attain peace. This naturalization of brutality, of the "continuation of politics by other (armed) means,"
needs to be integrated into any decolonial anti-racist feminist
analysis of violence. If we subscribe to the idea that societies are inevitably swamped with violence, it becomes totally
illusory to imagine a post-violent society and a decolonial and
anti-racist feminist politics of protection.

Following the Indigenous women of Central and South
America, I defend a de-patriarchalization and a decolonization
of protection; an alternative to patriarchal and State protection, this vast domain invested by the State, private militias, the
police, the courts, the economy, and civilizational feminism;[7] a
politics inspired by experiences in which communities, activist
groups, and health, legal, and education professionals have
reinvested the field of protection. Demonstrating that State
and neoliberal politics of protection are racialized does not
mean that bourgeoise women are not the targets of battering,
rape, and murder. But questioning protection through the lens
of class, race, and heteronormativity broadens our field of
action. This book thus takes an opposite view to carceral and
punitive feminism, which, according to Elizabeth Bernstein's
definition designates a branch of feminism that is in favor of
extending the penal sphere and calling for the criminalization
of certain acts, without questioning who is criminalized.[8]

The patriarchy is understood here as a structure of domination, which men engage with differentially. Heads of State
have adopted a "soft," feminist, and humanist patriarchy that

contrasts sharply with a vulgar, racist, homophobic, transphobic patriarchy that boasts of grabbing women "by the pussy,"[9] and is contemptuous of State institutions. Yet both pursue the same neoliberal politics, both defend the extractivist economy, both persist in perpetuating the West's grand narrative of infinite progress, which we know is historically founded on the exploitation of the people and resources of the Global South. These two patriarchies share the same contempt for the working classes (but lie to them differently), the same desire to be idolized, and the same will to rein in institutions.

I

Neoliberal Violence

Feminist movements and the rise of neoliberalism

Debates within feminism on the ties between patriarchy and the State, or between patriarchy and capitalism remain ongoing. Very early on, there were feminists who challenged the notion that the police and courts operate the same way for all women. Conceived to describe a supposedly homogeneous reality, the concept of "women" highlights the global nature of a form of oppression while at the same time masking the differences in its administering. In the 1970s, feminist movements in the Global South and in the North organized against the patriarchal State and against male chauvinism, virilism, and sexism in political parties, trade unions, and social movements. They rewrote the history of women's struggles, resituating their place in the revolutionary and anti-colonial movements, highlighting the entanglement of women's exploitation and that of the land and peoples, between imperialism and women's vulnerabilization. They debated sexualities, bodies, and representations. In the South and in the North, feminists questioned a Western feminist ideology that saw itself as universalist and claimed to speak in the name of all women. Dissensions emerged during international forums between this Western feminism and feminisms that, particularly in the South, insisted on the connections between capitalism, imperialism, racism, and the oppression of women, and on the way in which social class and forms of racialization interact. At the NGO Forum during the third World Conference on Women in Nairobi in 1985, this position was clearly formulated by Angela Davis, who declared:

in order truly to be an activist in the fight for women's equality, we have to recognize that women are oppressed as women, but we are also oppressed because of our racial and national backgrounds, we are also oppressed because of our class background. And there are those who might say, "Let's forget about race and class, we're all sisters. Let us join hands and across races, across classes." Well, I think we should join hands across races, across classes, but the specificity of our specific oppression must be recognized and acknowledged. And our struggles are not the same struggles.[1]

Maureen Reagan, President Ronald Reagan's daughter, sent to represent the women of the United States "does not represent me," Davis stated, adding that the appointment of the first woman to the United States Supreme Court (Sandra Day O'Connor) "was not a victory to the masses of women, ... it was a defeat," as she voted against abortion rights. Feminist agendas thus inevitably differed. In the 1970s and 1980s, Black, Chicana, African, Asian, and "Third World" feminist intellectuals and activists theorized the entanglement of oppressions.[2] In response, universities and governmental or international institutions added gender studies, feminist studies, women's studies to their curriculums. Feminists saw this inclusion as an institutionalization that ultimately risked weakening their struggles. While impossible to sum up here, these decades of intense theoretical work and mobilization brought progress in women's lives in both the South and North. What was clearly visible by the late 1970s was that there were *several* feminisms, some rooted in anti-imperialist and anti-racist struggles, defending radical, emancipatory feminism, others were reformist, others fighting to enter the army, the world of finance, and so on. While there were some circulations between radical feminism and reformist feminism, the former rejected any alliance with State feminism. Although political parties, unions, and social movements, which pushed back against any challenge to their male chauvinism, finally accepted a form of feminism, the links between racism and sexism remained marginalized. But governments and institutions gradually realized their interest in coopting a form of feminism, given women's massive entry into the wage labor market. In the 1980s, a civilizational and universalist feminism managed to impose itself internationally, minoritizing feminisms of combat that nonetheless did not disappear. The debate on the ties between patriarchy, capitalism, and State protectionism were far from over.

During these decades came another profound upheaval: neoliberalism. This stage of capitalism led to the privatization of public goods and services; the deregulation of finance, and the guarantee of high short-term profit margins for shareholders; the application of technical solutions to social problems; the creep of market rhetoric to legitimize profitability and flexibility norms, and to neutralize all opposition; and the exacerbation of extractivism. Driven by market logics, the structural adjustment programs imposed by international institutions on the Global South had devastating consequences, particularly for working-class racialized women and for Indigenous peoples. Even though, by 1975, "based on the figures, women showed that policies based uniquely on the liberal economic model were harmful to sustainable development and even more so to African women,"[3] few French feminist economists showed any interest in the consequences of these restructuration phenomena on women in the Global South.[4] Or rather, to put it differently, the effects of neoliberalism did not deeply permeate feminist theory in France, with the exception of a few groups linked to the far-left. This "conceptual silence" no doubt explains feminists' difficulty in revising their universalist theory later on. They ignored these policies' impact not only on the women of the African continent, but also on the so-called French Overseas Territories—Guadeloupe, Guiana, Kanaky-New Caledonia, Martinique, Mayotte, Polynesia, and Réunion Island—where, already in the 1960s, the government's de-industrialization policy caused unemployment, which the government then responded to with a mass emigration policy, notably of young women. For those behind the structural adjustment programs, it was for women to bear the brunt of the crisis of capitalism, and for the decisions taken by governments of the South under the constraint of economic measures, or following the abandonment of Independence programs. In the North, factory closures, and notably those that employed women (textiles, appliances, and so on), the development of service and care industries massively employing racialized women, underpaying them, and offering no stability, and the development of part-time work in which 80 percent of jobs are held by women, all led to far greater precarity. The gradual entry into the political vocabulary of the terms "insecurity" and "hazardous" contributed to justifying more police, more control, more surveillance, and less protection.

It is not so much that systemic violence is new—the long history of genocides, massacres, pillaging, and destruction prove the contrary, and capitalism has always had a colonial, racial, globalizing, and imperialist dimension—but hyperglobalization and the exacerbation of its extractivist logics have had an extremely negative impact on the life expectancy of vast populations. Achieved through struggle, progress in the fields of education, health, and training have been undermined, particularly in the Global South. Although people there now die in fewer numbers at birth and live a little longer, they breathe more polluted air, drink more polluted water, and are more often victim to epidemics, debt, the collapse of health and education services, and the consequences of extractivism-related climate change. Feminists reacted differently to these upheavals. In the North, a State and so-called "universalist civilizational" feminism developed, unperturbed by security-based and imperialist policies. This feminism operated a pacification of the "women's cause," which soon no longer represented something to fear for those in power. If in 1978, during a rape trial in Aix-en-Provence that mobilized feminists and led to the 1980 law that for the first time clarified what constitutes the crime of rape in France, the French press could still run the headline, "Openly or Secretly Feminist Women are Terrorists";[5] by the 1990s, the women's cause became not only what marketing calls talking points, but also a new object of public policy. Pacified, "gender equality" could enter government.

Against this pacifying feminism which had become complicit with capitalism and patriarchy, certain feminists persisted in analyzing the entanglements, interactions, and intersections between multiple layers of oppression. Queer, Muslim, Indigenous feminists added their voices to these theories. In their view, gender-based and sexual violence could not be analyzed and combatted in isolation from a broader analysis of the conditions in which these forms of violence are unleashed. Violence, then, is "the logical consequence of an analysis that posits women's oppression and their being kept in the minority as a structural reality of the State."[6]

Gore capitalism, rape, and murder politics

The analysis of gender-based and sexual violence cannot be dissociated from an analysis of these profound transformations that have produced the world we live in today: acute inequality, wealth concentrated in the hands of the very few, the ever faster destruction of living conditions, and politics of murder and devastation. Separating the situation of women from a global context of the naturalization of violence perpetuates a divide that benefits patriarchy and capitalism, the question becoming that of identifying and punishing "violent men," and naturalizing the violence of the few without dismantling the structures that generate abominable violence. In a context in which, despite demanding drastic public budget cuts, neoliberalism encourages police reinforcement and greater spending on armies and prisons, is it not crucial to question requests for protection, as they are most frequently formulated?

Rape institutes virilist heteronormative domination. In the war that the State and capital wage against those fighting for justice and dignity, rape is a weapon in the hands of the State. Indeed, "The more militant anticapitalism and international solidarity became everyday features of U.S. antiracist activism, the more vehemently the state responded," individualizing revolts to better criminalize them.[7] Rape has always been a weapon of war (and of colonial war in particular); there is no colonization, no imperialist occupation without rape. It is also part of the arsenal deployed for the repression of social movements. Whether in Cairo, Santiago, Baghdad, or elsewhere, the police and the army commit rape and gender-based and sexual violence with complete impunity. This impunity goes a long way back; it is rooted in the ideology of colonial racial war. "We approached another village. I heard officer candidate P ... shout out to his section: 'Go ahead and rape but be discreet about it!' ... On return that night, I learned that a fifteen-year-old young Muslim girl had been raped by seven soldiers, another thirteen-year-old by three other men. That night, I cried my first tears as a man," Benoist Rey wrote in *Les Égorgeurs* (*The Cut-Throats*), his account of being a French soldier during the Algerian war.[8] In 2016, the United Nations finally admitted that its troops had committed rape in Haiti, the Democratic Republic of Congo, Ivory Coast, South Sudan, and Mali.[9]

The lack of research into sexual and sexist violence against men and boys in conflict and post-conflict situations hides the fact that it is more widespread than admitted. The intention is not in any way to minimize the massive prevalence of the rape of women, but to understand that, as a weapon of racial and virilist domination, rape aims to destroy women and girls, but also men and boys too. Although these cases are rarely studied for fear of belittling the rape of women, because men raping men often remains unspeakable, and finally because we lack the vocabulary to speak about it, incorporating the rape of racialized men, gay men, trans men, and male sex workers into the analysis of gender-based and sexual violence shows that rape is inseparable from imperialism and racism; it is inseparable from virilist heteronormative domination. In 2004, the report on the torture of Iraqi detainees at Abu Ghraib revealed that North American soldiers threatened and sodomized "a detainee with a chemical light and perhaps a broom stick."[10] That women were involved in sexually torturing Muslim men came as no surprise within the arsenal of imperialist practices. Indeed, "the explicit use of women in military interrogations, precisely because they are women, in order to provoke anguish in men indeed corresponds to an authorized tactic known as 'the territorial extension' of the female soldier."[11] In addition to an Orientalist vision of Islam came a "State instrumentalization of sexual identity, sexuality, and sexual difference."[12] Women's participation in mechanisms of domination poses ethical and political questions. Female aggression cannot be the "result of their psychosis or their victimization alone," artist Coco Fusco writes, continuing: "neoconservative ideology promises all those willing to abandon their identification with minorities' 'special interests' access to political power and, at the same time, capitalizes—economically, especially—on women and minorities' presence, and on the sexual or ethnic difference that this clearly manifests."[13] Iraqi prison survivors spoke of forced sexual intercourse by the anus and mouth, of beatings to the genitals (and castration), of forced sexual intercourse by the perpetrator in all orifices of the body (for example, the nose, ear, mouth, and anus), and the insertion of objects, such as sticks and guns, in several orifices. Prison and camp survivors in Congo recounted having been forced by soldiers to watch wives, daughters, or other members of the family being raped, and/ or of being forced to sexually assault their mothers, daughters, or other family members.[14] In 2014, US Senate hearings revealed that CIA officers had used rectal feeding on "CIA detainees" in Guantanamo, who were "subjected to involuntary rectal feeding and rectal hydration, which included two bottles of Ensure"; "detainee Majid Khan was administered by enema his 'lunch tray' consisting of hummus, pasta with sauce, nuts and raisins' [which was] 'pureed and rectally infused'."[15] This procedure, an officer declared, was an effective "means of behavior control" as, according to doctors, it ensured a "'total control' over detainees."[16] "Normative masculinity at the service of the State and its political and economic mapping" was quite simply turned into a "potential war machine."[17] Another US Senate report of the same year listed "some of the health problems that Mustafa al-Hawsawi suffers from, clearly related to a 'rectal exam' carried out with 'excessive force' when he was a detainee in a secret prison in Afghanistan."[18] It continued: "The CIA files indicate that one of the detainees, Mustafa al-Hawsawi, was later diagnosed as suffering from chronic hemorrhoids, anal fissure, and symptomatic rectal prolapse." Mustafa al-Hawsawi was a victim of anal rape during his detention by the CIA, and the prolonged effects of the bodily harm he was subjected to were crucial at the time of his transfer to a secret prison in Lithuania in 2005. The Lithuanian authorities refused to provide healthcare for Mustafa al-Hawsawi and other prisoners' serious ailments, and the United States were forced to call on the services of other governments for this care.[19]

The European States that harbored the CIA's secret prisons were complicit in these rapes. In France in 2017, Théo Luhaka, a young Black 22-year-old wounded in the rectal area by a policeman's telescopic truncheon, was condemned to life-long medical treatment.[20] Finally, in her study carried out in Bangladeshi camps into the rape of Rohingya men, Sarah Chynoweth noted that "Stigma often prevents Rohingya men and boys from speaking up, while many aid groups aren't asking the right questions to find out—leaving ... male survivors of sexual violence with little help."[21] The needs of male survivors are largely unrecognized and ignored, she remarked. In the humanitarian sector, these rapes raise a wider debate about "whether gender-based violence programs should focus primarily on women and girls, who face additional risk in crises, or also better include men, boys, and the LGBTI community."[22] For the wife of one survivor in the Congo, "you touch a man like that, or a woman like that, it's the same thing";[23] men are raped after their wives and daughters have been raped by the same men.[24] Communities' reactions to the rape of women and men is not the same. Women are often rejected, seen as spoiled goods, but male rape is also a weapon of destruction: "They rape men to humiliate us, show the power that they have to capture everything and everybody, destroy men, masculinity and our culture, destroy families, show men that they are weak and don't have any power to protect themselves and their families."[25] In case it need be repeated, discussing male rape does not in any way diminish the horror of the rape of women nor its systemic nature. But the fact that its role in torture and the system of domination is increasingly recognized, and that anal torture is denounced, contributes to an analysis of rape as the expression of power. Brute, cruel violence is a form of government, a regime of existence. For academic and activist Sayak Valencia, "gore capitalism" creates this regime of existence. In this necro-empowerment, the injunction to hyperconsumerism produces an extreme brutality; staying alive is measured by the capacity to inflict death on others.[26] Gore capitalism weaponizes "masculinity" to serve its necropolitical project. The "decol-onization of necropolitical masculinity" is thus a "first step to denecropoliticize and depatriarchalize our country," writes Valencia. The rebellious young man, the *narco* (other figures also come to mind here) who has the

material resources to fight an armed revolution, as Frantz Fanon would have liked, ... does not do so, and will not do so, for he is seduced by the colonial apparatus imposed by neoliberalism and sees himself more as an entrepreneur in the service of Euro-patriarchal logics of the self-made man than as a rebel. The narco does not want to be a revolu-tionary, he wants to be an entrepreneur. As we know, the entrepreneur wants to access the advantages of neoliberal-ism's whitewashing.[27]

Violence gives meaning to an existence programed for prema-ture death; it allows people to exist for an ephemeral moment, having access to what has become proof of existence. Here, women, trans people, queer people, male and female sex workers are simply bodies to rape, traffic, torture, kill. All these killable bodies are feminized in the sense that they are put at the disposal of domination: babies, children, teenagers, adults, the elderly; no age group, sex, or gender escapes this economy: "Murder is now conceived as a transaction, extreme violence as a legitimate tool, torture as an ultra-profitable exercise and display of power."[28] Valencia's analysis adds a feminist element to the perspective of the South that is lacking in Achille Mbembe's theory of necropolitics. These practices exist in France; they do not belong to the colonial past, they are present in the policies that consist of

> closing borders, barring uteruses, deporting foreigners and emigrants, banning them from working, accessing housing, healthcare, eradicating Judaism, Islam, locking up or exterminating Black people, homosexuals, transexuals ... Ultimately, the aim is to explain to us that certain bodies of the Republic should not have access to governmental techniques, depending on their national, sexual, racial, religious identity, that there are bodies born to govern and others that should remain the objects of governmental practice.[29]

The violence of the market and of precarity

The notions of vulnerability and precarity must be handled with caution, for they are employed by governments and international institutions that instigate health and social approaches destined to marginalize the vulnerable and invisibilize the processes at play in the spread of precarity. Rather than apprehending the mechanisms that produce vulnerabilities, an ideology of self-entrepreneurship, of the self as capital to be fructified is advocated, the failure to become one's own entrepreneur becoming the sign of a lack of will *to make it*. The psychic life of neoliberalism is based on the notion that success is strictly one's own making, that egotism is the motor of excellence and wealth. Ayn Rand provided this ideology its philosophy: any vulnerability or sign of weakness is to be eradicated as an obstacle on the path of talented and motivated people—exclusively white men. This ideology encourages an entirely individual, often patriarchal form of responsibility, and bolsters a conservative nationalism that is also often patriarchal. The weak hereby (unsurprisingly) become part of the new civilizing mission, the target of a paternalistic philanthropy determined to prevent any emergence of a new conception of inhabiting, of being human in the world. The vulnerable are relegated to contemporary zones of nonbeing—that vast, "extraordinarily sterile and arid region, an utterly naked declivity where an authentic upheaval can be born,"[30] zones in which exploitation reigns, in which the use of violence prevails, in which politics coincide with murder, and extinction becomes the norm. While neoliberalism accuses individuals of their own failure, neofascism looks for scapegoats, but the two ideologies join in denying the role of the State and capitalism's institutional violence. The analysis of practices of dehumanization and vulnerabilization demonstrate that we inevitably need to think and act along several temporalities, repairing past politics of dehumanization and vulnerablization (including the still very recent past), and their contemporary and emerging forms, whose impacts we can already measure. This means, in the ruins of the present, discovering and collectively experimenting with people's practices of humanization and devulnerabilization. Black, African, and Indigenous feminist theories come to mind, notably those involving care, solidarity, and the environment, as do practices and discourses of hope, of utopia, from which real visions are born. We do not have an "elsewhere" completely protected from systemic violence, but we do have a map of fault lines, of interstices, of poorly guarded, opaque spaces in which to deploy practices that are not founded on calculation and market value.

This is to say that we need to resist an entire economy of exhaustion in which "the pillaging and plundering of the feminine" is articulated in two ways: on the one hand, "an unprecedented corporal destruction," and on the other, "the trafficking and commercialization of what these bodies can offer, pushed to its extreme limit. Never has the predatory occupation of female or feminine bodies reached such a level."[31] Having demonstrated that commodification now concerns all elements of the living, theoretical approaches highlight the extent to which a politics of death is hidden behind the discourse of modernity, progress, the market. It is also necessary to recognize the seductive power of such rhetoric, even for individuals and groups victim to these ideologies; being excluded from power does not "necessarily [ward off] its spells."[32]

If, in the past, colonial violence allowed the rapid acquisition of wealth, gore capitalism has turned it into a global strategy. "McDonalds cannot flourish without McDonnell-Douglas [the defense contractor],"[33] writes Valencia; one could add there would be no Accor or Bolloré (French corporations) without *la Françafrique*, the sphere of influence that French imperialism carved out in its former African colonies. Thwarted access to hyperconsumerism results in an unending spiral of negativity, not only of material deprivation, but of mental suffering and the shame of being differentiated, of being poor, and encourages descent into committing acts of violence. With the same desire to analyze the way in which the vocabulary of sexist and racial brutality materializes and becomes consensual even for those who are also its targets, South African psychologist Ivan Katsere suggested rejecting the notion of xenophobia to describe the deadly violence carried out against migrants in his country in August 2019.[34] For him, this violence demonstrated the ideological power of racism and its capacity as a structure to be embodied and enacted by Black people against Black people. This racialization proves colonialism's degree of "perfection," that is, the full circle of the racist dehumanization phenomenon that has Black people maintain "other" Black people on the fringes of society and exterminate them in a manner conceived for, and by, colonialism.

From gender to patriarchal capitalism

If consumerism and the ideology of "progress" have such powers of seduction, what can be said of notions forged in struggle then absorbed into capitalism, such as gender? If, as Karina Bidaseca states, "gender, like race, is a powerful fiction,"[35] what to make of this concept? What to make of the expressions "gender equality" and "gender relations," which have "long influenced world society in its entirety, even if [gender] is not represented in the same way everywhere and even if, on closer inspection, huge differences can be observed"?[36] Should we not, rather, continue to analyze the way in which the concepts of "femininity" and "masculinity" are the "pillars of the goods-producing patriarchy"?[37] How to highlight the mechanisms of "complicit masculinity" that, for Martha Zapata Galindo, characterize men who do not necessarily advocate the hegemonic prototype (of virilism), but who nonetheless readily receive the dividends of patriarchy, enjoy all the advantages that result from discrimination against women, and, with no particular effort, benefit from material advantages, prestige, and authority?[38]

In 2018, Black women launched a strike in the US giant McDonald's North American branches under the following slogan: "Hold your burgers, hold your fries, keep your hands off my thighs!"[39] Investigations confirmed endemic sexual harassment and racism in the famous chain:

In Durham, North Carolina, one female employee paid seven dollars fifty an hour described a "work environment steeped in explicit sexual language, sexual harassment and racism." One of her bosses proposed her a threesome. Another gave her salacious nicknames. A third kept making passes at her, despite her explicit refusals. After she reported one of her harassers, her colleagues made fun of her. Her young 17-year-old brother, also employed in the same restaurant, was the target of homophobic remarks.[40]

For the McDonald's strikers, the fight against sexual violence went hand-in-hand with that for better wages and work conditions; one of their tweets was perfectly explicit about this: "A moment of remembrance for Yasmin Fernandez at today's @ McDonald's sexual harassment strike. Yasmin was a leader in the movement for fast food workers' rights who passed away last year working alone in an overheated kitchen in @Panda-Express."[41] In France, Black women strikers at the Hotel Ibis Batignolles (Accor Group) also made the connection between economic exploitation, racial harassment, and sexual violence. In 2019, during the annual march protesting violence against women, a few words handwritten on a banner by one of the strikers summed this up: "Exploiting hotel maids is sexist violence too." The relation between economic exploitation, racism, class contempt, and gender and sexual violence is clear. It became tragically even more so when, in March 2017, a maid working in the Paris Ibis hotel (employed by the subcontractor TNF TEFID) was raped by the hotel director—which, in January 2020, Accor still refused to admit.[42] The industries that employ, offer unstable conditions to, and exploit racialized women—the fast-food, hotel, and care industries, and sweatshops—all have extremely high rates of sexual and racial harassment.

A semblance of protection: three accounts of everyday violence

In the face of this barrage of systemic violence, State mechanisms and discourses of "protection" struggle to dissimulate their underlying logics of racialization. One only need think of the insurmountable discrepancy between discourses on the protection of women and the vulnerable on the one hand, and the measures and laws that brutally exacerbate precarity and institutional violence on the other. These contrasts trace a line between those who can and must be protected, and those who cannot or must not be. This division between a humanity considered entitled to protection and those (almost by nature) excluded from it to me remains a tangible division that structures the social world. Conversations about women's protection from systemic violence cannot adopt a binary female victim/male perpetrator approach, in which the role of protector is entrusted to the male, rapist State, femicides being "the ultimate expression of a continuum of power which begins with the pervasiveness of social and economic inequalities, sexual harassment, sexual violence, and the sexist representations that structure the social imagination and public space."[43]

To better illustrate the logics of this distinction between those "to protect" and the other, sacrificeable people, I would like to recount three apparently ordinary personal experiences. First, a trip to a major—prestigious, as the usual terminology goes—liberal university on the east coast of the United States where I was invited to give a seminar in the Fall of 2017. Immediately on my arrival in a country that had been run for a year by a sexist, racist, homophobic, and fascistic president, I was struck by the contrast on the one hand between the overblown multiplication of discourses and tools of protection on the campus to make it a secure and protected space, especially for the female students and women working there, the almost daily reminder of these measures that, at all hours of the day and night, justified the deployment of a private campus police—who were incidentally always very friendly—and, on the other, the Trump government's unleashing of brutality, which, in its measures and declarations, more than ever bared the imperialism and heteronormative racial capitalism that, historically, characterize the United States. Protection on campus manifested itself not only through a display of security, but also by the cleanliness of the place, the manicured lawns, the facilitated access to all sorts of services, the diversity of the cultural offer, the number of food-trucks proposing organic vegan food, and the beauty of the buildings. And yet, my hijab-wearing, Black, queer, Latinx students did not feel safe. One of them—an Iraqi refugee active in the BDS movement—told me about the Islamophobic attacks she was subjected to and her feeling of isolation. On the campus, a few, mainly queer women's groups had suggested organizing themselves into self-defense groups, but this idea had been strongly discouraged by the authorities, who recommended that they speak to the university's security officer, legal services, and psychologists. At the same time, in the wake of the #MeToo movement, women's testimonies were circulating online, albeit in closed circuit, denouncing harassment in academia: female PhD candidates forced to change their subjects, supervisor, or university; candidates forgoing a position or a promotion because they were proposed in return for sexual favors; female academics describing the fear, isolation, or depression in which they found themselves. For racialized female academics, racism and sexism combined. A campus where women can circulate without fear of being harassed is an improvement, one might counter, and I recognize that it is possible to defend this position, but I cannot embrace this sentiment of protection without thinking about the insecurity and financial precarity suffered by my hijab-wearing and Black female students, universities' privatization policies, and the violence that was being exerted unbridled off campus. At the same time that everything was being done to produce a sentiment of security, I saw the campus as an enclave, and that was not all that reassuring. In the nearby town, the ravaged neighborhoods inhabited by racialized communities made it absolutely clear that this protection was not available to everyone. This fashioning of space into enclaves in the name of security revealed the extent to which privatized or State protection comes on the condition of accepting norms requiring obedience to the segregated order. At a time when wars waged by the United States in Iraq and Afghanistan were exacerbating vulnerability for women and children,[44] when Black Lives Matter was revealing the dangers of public space for Black people, when State racism was becoming increasingly virulent, when children were being torn from their parents at the Mexican border, some even disappearing from the records, this discourse and this implementation of protection for the few exposed the limits of a politics of protection blind to race, misogyny, and capitalism. What this division of space revealed is that the outside world is hostile, that (racialized) men are threatening, that the streets are unsafe, and that in order to be protected from all these dangers, we must entrust our protection to those whose profession is "protection" (private security and surveillance companies, militias, police). Violence was met with the creation of spaces surveilled by private police, where the campus was cut off from the outside world and its dangers, yet this construction of enclaves in the form of guarded residencies, private police, the rise in surveillance equipment and measure of control only reinforce social and racial segregation and, ultimately, revealed the fragility of these forms of protection.

This politics of protection has become an enormous, militarized business where experts boast their products' performance and their surveillance tools' ability to detect "abnormal or suspect behavior: a person who stumbles, a pickpocket who can be tracked from one camera to another in a shop or town. The purpose here is not identify the person, but to recognize their silhouette, clothes, whether they are wearing glasses or have a beard."[45] Ignoring the impact of these technologies of surveillance and control, which are mainly dominated by white heteronormative males, simply perpetuates the chronic violence that goes with these measures. Combatting violence against women without taking into account the militarization of protection, the construction of dangerous classes and races, legitimizing recourse to evermore surveillance and control by private companies subcontracted by the State, or by the State itself, is to be complicit in the prevalence of violence as protection.

The second experience I wish to relate took place in 2019 in France when the media, government, and political representatives adopted the idea of femicide. It was henceforth acknowledged that the murder of a woman because she was a woman warranted specific mention. Articles were then regularly published, debates took place, the government was called on because every two days, a woman dies at the hands of her husband, partner, or ex. The newspaper *Libération* decided to report every femicide. In early September, a group of young women in Paris began pasting up slogans in black letters on sheets of white paper: "Daddy killed Mommy," "She left him, he killed her," "Femicide: we no longer want to count our dead," "Gaëlle, pregnant, stabbed to death by her ex. 24th femicide," or, playing on the famous words inscribed on the pediment of the Panthéon in Paris, "To the murdered women, the ungrateful homeland."[46] In his October 2 report on the draft bill that he tabled, and after recalling femicide and domestic violence figures in France, the right-wing Les Républicains MP Aurélien Pradié repeated the findings of his colleague Philippe Dunoyer, who in the same year during a debate on funding to the French Overseas Territories, argued that "violence against women is more widespread in the Overseas Territories than in metropolitan France and the rate of the worst acts of aggression above average." A racialized geography was surreptitiously slipped into the parliamentarians' speeches; if, indeed, the number of femicides is higher in the "Overseas Territories," the terms employed were those of a culturalized frame of analysis. In the parliamentarians' mind, "overseas" men are obviously racialized, and thus, quite logically, naturally more violent than the average white man, and this without ever addressing the social, economic, and political context of extreme neocolonial violence. Next, drawing on the positive effects of a law against sexual violence adopted in Spain, and acknowledging the shortcomings of judicial decisions in France, the MP called for a strengthening of judges' power, a faster implementation of their decisions, and the application of measures guaranteeing that restraining or protection orders be pronounced against current or former partners. The law, which prescribes that domestic abusers obligatorily wear "an electronic bracelet that geolocalizes and keeps current and former violent partners away by triggering an alert, according to a perimeter set by a judge," was adopted on October 15, 2019. The government then organized a *Grenelle des violences conjugales*, or public consultation on domestic abuse.[47] On November 24, shortly before its conclusions were announced, in an effort to influence the decisions to come, rallies against femicide were held in several French cities at the call of the #NousToutes (#All of Us Women) collective and backed by 70 organizations, political parties, trade unions, and associations. "The government is going to have to meet the expectations of this unprecedented social mobilization," declared Caroline De Haas, member of the #NousToutes collective, demanding that a "billion euros be put on the table" to combat violence, and that prevention and training measures be announced. "At the moment, violence is dealt with once it has happened, a bit like if in road safety, we only dealt with road accident victims, without taking any prior action. There needs to be a change of direction," she urged.[48] The government, to whom this demand was addressed, had spelled out the content of its feminist policies as soon as it came to power—a ministry headed by a straight-talking, dynamic young woman, highly present on social media, in charge of a feminist summer school where a young hijab-wearing woman was prevented from speaking by a feminist audience who then, albeit in irritation, listened without interruption to a white man lecturing them for twenty minutes.[49] This government also had a civilizational feminist foreign policy; a president not hesitating to repeatedly state his feminism, and, at the same time, a president, his government, and its parliamentary majority who, through their decisions, have made the rich richer and the poor poorer, the lives of working-class and racialized women harder and more precarious, obstructed the freedom of the press, lied, persisted in portraying the hijab as a sign of female submission, and encouraged their police forces to employ brutal, harmful, mutilating or lethal methods in complete impunity. It is of course necessary to continue demanding that the State provide a budget and means for women fleeing violence, but should we not, in the light of this government's decisions, ask ourselves on what criteria it bases its politics of protection? What about the women refugees sleeping rough in our streets, who, because of European laws, are confronted with all sorts of violence? What about the women *Gilets Jaunes* who lost an eye?[50]

The third event I would like to mention is the mobilization of the mothers of a group of 162 schoolboys from Mantes-la-Jolie, a small town to the south of Paris classed as one of the poorest communes in the country. Following the boys' detention on December 6, 2018, by police equipped with helmets, truncheons, and shields—police who forced them to kneel in rows in silence for hours, their hands behind their heads or backs, eyes down, their bookbags on their backs, while one of the officers declared in a video that went viral, "This is what a well-behaved class looks like"[51]—the teens' mothers organized. In the collective they set up, they interpreted the images of their kneeling children "as symptomatic, not a gaffe, that is, as a moment of truth for this teetering Republic that only keeps its poor and descendants of the colonized in place with truncheons, Tasers, Flash Balls, and prison. Today, like last year, preventative civil war is the only measure that the government is capable of to protect itself from its own crises."[52] While some political figures considered this police violence excessive and unjustifiable,[53] others saw nothing wrong with it. The Socialist leader Ségolène Royal[54] even considered this humiliation and violence a good lesson: "There weren't just high-schoolers among these youths. There were rioters too, who, with unbelievable savagery, began lighting fires all over Mantes. But let's be a bit effective and concrete. It did these youths no harm to know what law and order and what the police are, to behave. It's something they'll remember. And it's not bad to teach them a sense of reality."[55] Thierry Laurent, director of the office of the Prefect of the Yvelines department, for his part stated: "These images are unquestionably harsh and surprising. They nonetheless need to be put in the context of the violence that these individuals carried out in Mantes-la-Jolie for three days." He went further, invoking the fact that some of the adolescents had come out hooded and armed: "There was no intention to humiliate," he said, insisting on the police officers' "professionalism."[56] The desire to humiliate was nonetheless well and truly clear, for it is obvious that a hundred or so high schoolers from white bourgeois families in Paris would not have been forced to kneel for hours by the police, their hands behind their heads, nor would the children and their parents' complaints have been rejected. What was thus revealed in Mantes-la-Jolie that day in December was the continuation of a racial colonial politics that refuses these children the right to be children and which, inflicting humiliation, aims to discipline racialized working-class communities. "Worried to know that [their] children [were] no longer protected,"[57] the "151 Mothers and Women of Mantes-la-Jolie and Mantois" stood up "to police arbitrariness" and declared: "We, moms of the projects, moms of the neighborhoods, moms of the kneeling children of Mantes-la-Jolie, we no longer accept this state of permanent injustice. We want just one thing: Peace."[58] By using the word "moms," these women put this word sometimes considered retrograde back into public discourse; here "mom" indicated a posture of protection and the reappropriation of a function historically denied to racialized women: maternity. These mothers distinguished between a State politics of protection that protects the interests of the white bourgeoisie, and a politics of protection that the community takes responsibility for in a demilitarized public space, and which guarantees racialized children the same protection as all children. They criticized the discourse that considers racialized parents to be bad parents, incapable of disciplining their children, of ensuring they are "well behaved," and do well at school, the discourse that considers these children to be criminals in-the-making. By speaking of peace, they outlined a politics of the peaceable in neighborhoods placed under police surveillance.

The multiplication of measures, laws, and declarations concerning the protection of women and children alongside increased precarity, vulnerability, and violence against women and children is not paradoxical. It is the result of political choices that draw a line between women who have the right to protection and those who are excluded, between children who have a right to childhood as conceived by modern psychology (that is, protected from the violence of adults or from police violence) and children whose childhood is criminalized—those children who the police and courts apprehend as adults, who are excluded from the education system, the young teenagers who have to prove their age to be considered minors, the racialized young women whose sexuality or religious practice are mocked and scorned. When protection is subjected to racial, class, gender, and sexual criteria, it contributes in its logic and its application to domination. One politics serves another; in other words, the racist and patriarchal State's politics of protection requires these distinctions between who has the right to protection and who does not.

2

Race, Patriarchy, and the Politics of Women's Protection

Femo-imperialism and the protection of women of the Global South

In France and the French post-colonies, universalist civilizational feminism has helped incorporate women's protection into the "civilizing mission." The frequency with which sexual aggression cases are seized upon by these "feminists" as an opportunity to link them with racist narratives continues to attest to this. In 2011, former Socialist Women's Rights Minister Yvette Roudy, who qualified Dominique Strauss-Khan's rape of Nafissatou Diallo as "a political affair," was thus unable to refrain from concluding: "It's no accident that gang rape is a weapon of war, a way for young thugs from the hoods to cowardly assert themselves through gang rapes."[1] In what was supposed to be a denunciation of sexism in politics, why conflate this powerful man, the head of the IMF, who was totally convinced of his impunity, and the youth of working-class neighborhoods, other than to yet again lend credence to the idea that the greatest danger comes from young men of color from poor neighborhoods? And this at the very instance that a Black immigrant woman was raped by a powerful white man who was immediately defended by his peers, who called it "a bit of skirt-lifting with the servants."[2] In a more recent interview, in answer to the question, "Thirty years ago, you compared France's political parties to nineteenth-century English clubs: male, elitist, and private. Is that still so?", Yvette Roudy replied, "No, it has changed, but it's a fact: we are very behind in France. We have to contend with the weight of the traditions of our immigrant population's countries of origin."[3] Again, racialized communities bore the responsibility for French society's macho and misogynistic attacks. Its backwardness in terms of women's rights was attributed to communities deemed alien to the Nation. We can only but draw the obvious conclusions: according to this vision (of those considered the most legitimate), becoming a French woman presupposes the exclusion of women and men who are French citizens but condemned to always being foreigners. This slippage that links the denunciation of abuse, of a rape, with the presence of racialized people in France reinforces the idea that racialized men are a threat to (white) women's freedom.

The civilizational approach to women's protection also serves as an argument of French foreign policy. Speaking before the UN in 2019, French President Emmanuel Macron laid out France's talking points:

Women and girls are the first to be affected by poverty, conflict, and the effects of global warming; they are the first victims of sexist and sexual violence, which too often stops them from circulating freely, from working, from disposing of their bodies as they choose. It is time that our world stops victimizing women and at last carves them out the place they deserve: that of being leaders too![4]

"France," he added, is implementing "active and resolutely feminist diplomacy"; accordingly, his government committed to allocating "50% of public development aid to gender equality measures."[5] These programs, he added, target both "the emancipation of African women," the "fight against female genital mutilation," cyber-bullying, and female education. Combatting female genital cutting is one of Western feminism's obsessions, for, *in their view*, sexual mutilation is the sign of backwardness and cruelty toward women by uncivilized men. This obsession does not take into account the grassroots struggles of African women, nor the fact pointed out by Fati N'Zi Hassane:

> almost all over Africa, female genital mutilation is on the decline. This decline is particularly striking in East Africa, where the rate of under fifteen-year-old girls mutilated fell from 71% to 8% between 1995 and 2016, according to UNICEF. This decline is unfortunately considerably less visible in West Africa and in the Horn of Africa, the two regions most concerned by this inhuman practice widespread throughout the Sahelian belt from Mauritania to Somalia. Nonetheless, there too, the figures of the United Nations Population Fund (UNFPA) regional office for West and Central Africa indicate a drastic change over the generations.[6]

For African women activists, the intervention of Western NGOs and governments is counterproductive: their practices, vocabulary, their way of intervening produce the opposite results to those intended—but it is true that referring to sexual mutilation guarantees media attention. France's "active and resolute feminist" policy aims to educate African women to become leaders—"locomotives," in short. To better serve its feminist policy, the French State, in the footsteps of North American foundations, decided to set up an investment fund for gender-equality projects. In August 2019, during the G7 summit in Biarritz, Emmanuel Macron announced the creation of this investment fund alongside Akinwumi Adesina, president of the African Development Bank, and the artist Angélique Kidjo:

> Basically, a real challenge for Africa is that there are two driving forces demographically speaking—women and men—and there is only one driving force that receives help—the men ... The other driving force is at a standstill because, in a lot of African countries, the women are refused access to land and property, which is a fundamental challenge, and this therefore means that they are not allowed access to credit. They cannot develop an activity and, in a lot of African countries, have no access to credit, to borrowing (apart from microcredits), and therefore to developing entrepreneurship.[7]

In July 2017, during a G20 summit, the same Macron had declared about the African continent: "When there are still countries today with seven to eight children per woman, you can spend billions of euros there, you won't stabilize a thing."[8] With these words, "Emmanuel Macron set the tone: his discourse was to be feminist, or rather femo-colonialist," wrote Elsa Dorlin, "as, by defending African women's rights and reproductive choices, the French president positioned himself as a knight in shining armor."[9] Femo-imperialism has definitively adopted the notion of gender (exclusively designating women, here, and taken as a single entity) and feminist formulae (freedom of movement, to dispose of one's body) to promote a politics of integrating African women into a banking and economic system dominated by the West, while at the same time continuing to position African women as responsible for the state of the continent. The vocabulary of twenty-first-century colonial feminism has thus emerged, borrowing from femo-colonialism and the ideology of neoliberal entrepreneurship: African women are thrifty and industrious; they are more highly educated than men; they act as good "heads of family"; they invest in sectors that benefit all of society (health, education), unlike African men who only invest "between 30 to 40%" in such sectors. The qualities that patriarchy perceives as feminine—being frugal, serious, thrifty—and which have justified women's inferior status, are translated here in economic terms. African women are given the task of alleviating the negative effects of crises caused by structural adjustment programs. Rather than reparation policies that would facilitate women's autonomy, they are invited to become debtors of the banking system. More debt is added to the debt that the peoples of the South must pay the States that impoverished them. This fact had not escaped North American foundations and investment funds before Macron. On April 4, 2019, the media informed us that, in the name of the Overseas Private Investment Corporation (OPIC),[10] Ivanka Trump was planning a trip to Africa to promote the "Invest in Women, Invest in the World" program. In its study, the OPIC observed that "women in developing countries" had become the principal factor in the increase in world consumption. It was thus time to take an interest in this phenomenon, all the more so because targeting women would guarantee economic prosperity and world stability. Sub-Saharan Africa—which regroups more educated and female entrepreneurs than any other continent—has naturally become a priority for the OPIC. The "world," the investment fund declared, could not neglect the multi-billion generative opportunity that the women of the Global South represent. Reducing the gender gap would add $28 trillion to global product by 2025, with the female economy soon to represent a market twice the size of India and China combined. Given that women of the Global South make up 73 percent of microcredit institutions' clientele,[11] we can understand the banks' and investment funds' interest. In response to the perspective according to which, from now to 2028, women consumers are set to control approximately $15 billion of world consumer spending, the OPIC produced a *gender-based* frame of analysis to judge all projects concerning women. How to understand the relationship between these neoliberal policies that claim to defend and promote the future of African women and the necro-economics that fragilize that very future? The fact that these two present/futures coexist—a world in which racialized women are free, entrepreneurial, and autonomous, and a fragmented, violent, devastating, destructive world, in other words, one rooted in the legacies of colonialism—makes apparent the cloak that veils the objectives of neoliberal capitalism: to make women and men bear the burden of hardship, discrimination, and vulnerabilities by promoting individualism. The aim of the Invest in Women, Invest in the World policy—a policy of integrating racialized women and women of the Global South as *added value*, as the object of investment by the finance world—is an act of pacification. The "female" gender as conceived by the West—an essentialized group, marked by biological difference—is used against the racialized "male gender"—there, too, an essentialized group, also marked by biological difference and race.

The genealogy of a hostile environment

While differences exist within all societies in their approaches to protection, it can be said that the patriarchal and capitalist State has reinforced these disparities, which have notably been racialized. In France, however, it is still very hard to study and publicly discuss the impact through the lens of race. While works on class differences are plentiful and have produced solid results, approaches based on race have been neglected. In this regard, it is simply astonishing the extent to which the realities of slavery are minimized, reduced to a simple memorial ritual, and colonization envisaged exclusively through the frame of representations, when slavery and colonization are in fact the very matrices of modernity. There is a profound denial of the ways in which centuries of colonial empire, enslavement, and post-enslavement have marked French society, its arts, literature, laws, political organizations, trade union and social movements, and feminisms. While the question of racial representations is now more or less accepted in the public debate, and even the object of major museum exhibitions, racism in political thought remains marginal. I yet again (as always), insist on the centrality of colonial slavery in the fabrication of vulnerability to a premature death, in the normative and racial notions of femininity and proper masculinity, in the invention of what constitutes the "good" family, the good maternities and paternities, in the construction of childhood, in the economy of the exhaustion of bodies and wealth.[12] Although the zones of immiseration are multiplying, North/South, centre/margins divisions remain, but within a globalization of deteriorated living conditions. Processes of the destruction of social life appeared in the South and racialized communities of the North in the 1970s, and spread there more rapidly. The people of the Global South have not only been dispossessed of their land, cut off from their resources, but have even been excluded as a respected labor force.[13] Acknowledging this is not to deny social class, it is to accept that race has marked the world. With regards to France, the Togolese economist Kako Nubukpo's observation that "the current mode of growth" maintains "Africa in the so-called 'colonial slavery' model,",[14] also applies to France's so-called "Overseas" territories, which are systematically excluded from analyses. Denouncing a so-called obsession with race in reference to the attention paid by activists and academics to processes of racialization thus amounts to pure calumny.[15]

A specialist of colonial slavery and processes of whitewash-ing, historian Catherine Hall has fittingly linked the grand narrative of the emergence of a "hostile environment" to non-white people in the UK: slavery plays a central role in this.[16] "Even committed antislavery activists like Granville Sharp were quite clear about the difference between white Britons and Africans: it was slavery that was the problem," Hall writes.[17] Black people's presence in England caused deep anxiety among whites, relationships between the sexes con-stituting one of the main aspects of this. In 1774, Edward Long, one of the most ardent proslavery advocates, alerted his readers to "the sexual dangers such proximity to 'the negro' [in the original] engendered." He wrote, "The lower class of women in *England* are remarkably fond of the blacks, for reasons too brutal to mention."[18] A dilution of "English" blood was to be feared:

> Thus, in the course of a few generations more, the English blood will become so contaminated with this mixture ... as even to reach the middle, and then the higher orders of the people, till the whole nation resembles the *Portuguese* and Moriscos in complexion of skin and baseness of mind. This is a venomous and dangerous ulcer, that threatens to disperse its malignancy far and wide, until every family catches infection from it.[19]

According to Catherine Hall, this hostile environment has never come to an end. In 1955, the grand hero of the English imperial narrative, Winston Churchill, toyed with adopting the slogan, "Keep England White." In 2012, while Minister of the Interior for the David Cameron government, Theresa May announced her wish to create "in Britain, a really hostile environment for illegal immigrants." In 2018, several hundred *Windrush*-generation immigrants—identified after the name of the ship that brought the first English-speaking Caribbean immigrants to the UK—and their descendants risked deportation.[20] The same processes play out in France. To say that there have never been racial laws in France is to ignore the history of anti-Semitism and anti-Black, anti-Muslim, anti-Roma racism. In 1776, the monarchy legislated on the presence of Black people in France. It feared an increase in requests for freedom from the enslaved on the grounds of the royal edicts of 1315, which stipulated that "no one may be a slave on French soil" and that "French soil frees the slave who lands on it." The same year, a royal commission advocated banning entry to Black people and forbade marriage between Black and white people, and even between Black people. The aim was to stymie requests for freedom from Black people brought to France by slave traders and the constitution of Black communities. On August 7, 1777, a *Police des Noirs* was set up, creating places to detain the enslaved in every French port while their owners were in France. As of January 11, 1778, all registered Black people had to carry an identification card (a *cartouche*) indicating their name, age, and their master's name, under the penalty of being sent back to the colonies. If Black people could not produce their *cartouche*, they were arrested and questioned. If the police were able to confirm their identity, the enslaved were freed but nonetheless taken to the depot for deportation and their owner obliged to pay a prescribed fine.[21] The French Revolution abolished these measures and, under the impetus of the slave insurrection that broke out in 1791 in the colony of Saint-Domingue (future Haiti), abolished slavery on February 4, 1794 (it had been abolished in Saint-Domingue in 1793). This abolition decree only entered into effect in Guadeloupe; in Bourbon (Réunion), Isle de France (Mauritius), Martinique (under English occupation), and Guiana, it was rejected by the slaveholders. Terrified by the Black insurrection in Saint-Domingue and the abolition of slavery in Guadeloupe, the slaver world prepared its offensive. In the early nineteenth century, slave owners from the French colonies who took refuge in the United States and the colonial lobby in France developed their arguments in favor of the restoration or maintaining of slavery. Their objective found support among the anti-revolutionaries and an ally in Napoleon Bonaparte. Anti-Black racism was at the heart of the propaganda for the restoration of slavery, which was justified by the behavior of the "Blacks of Guadeloupe," namely, "the major crimes that these Blacks have just defiled themselves with in their sinful resistance and rebellion," and "above all, the abominable use that the Blacks of Guadeloupe have made of freedom by taking up arms in patricide against the government of the Metropole, disobeying its orders, combatting its victorious troops with open force, destroying its factories, burning down towns and the countryside, and stamping out legitimate ownership." "The example of neighboring colonies where slavery subsists" offered "a striking contrast of prosperity, of domestic tranquility," where, furthermore, social harmony reigned, for the observing of "reciprocal duties" between masters and slaves "is the measure of happiness that belongs to each class."[22] There was no universal access to rights because Black people allegedly did not know how to put their freedom to good use, they would ruin the economy, and contest private property. What that author of this official document called "parricide" was the desire to overthrow a colonial power that guaranteed no protection against cruelty and the abuse of power, and to institute their own forms of protection.

In late March 1802, Baudry Deslozières' work *Les Égarements du nigrophilisme* (*The Follies of Negrophilism*) was published, in which the author wrote:

Despite our better will, we have come to recognize the natural evidence that their species is depraved, that theirs is the most imperfect class of humanity, the most somber, the most incapable of enlightenment, the most wicked, the most incorrigible. We have come to the conclusion that they are not made for the freedom of Whites, and their conduct thus far increasingly proves this truth.[23]

On May 16, 1802 (27 Floréal year X[24]), the government spokesperson, Adet, presented the draft law on the re-establishment of slavery before the Tribunat, insisting on its economic interest:

Whatever horror it inspires, [slavery] is useful in European societies' current organization; no people can abandon it without compromising the interests of the other nations … By letting yourselves be carried away by a sentiment that honors you … you risk sacrificing the interests of your country to Blacks by destroying an institution necessary to the colonies, which have themselves become necessary to our existence.[25]

The bill was adopted by the Tribunat by a majority of 54 votes to 27. The decree re-establishing slavery was issued on May 20, 1802: "In the name of the French people, Bonaparte, First Consul, proclaims the following decree law of the Republic, returned by the Corps législatif on 30 Floréal year X, in accordance with the proposition tabled by the government on 27 of the said month and transferred to the Tribunat on the same day."[26] Its first article was clear: "in the colonies restituted to France in application of the Treaty of Amiens of 6 Germinal year X, slavery will be maintained in accordance with the laws and regulations preceding 1789." The treaty was also declared to be in keeping with the law of the Republic. It was a Republic that restored racial laws with its "Order forbidding Blacks, Mulattos, and other people of color from entering the continental territory of the Republic without authorization. The 13 Messidor, year X of the unique and undividable Republic," which banned "all foreigners from bringing into the continental territory of the Republic any Blacks, Mulattos, or people of color, of one sex or the other," and forbade "any Black, Mulatto or other people of color, of one or other sex, who are not in service, to enter the continental territory of the Republic in future, for whatever cause and pretext whatsoever, unless they are carrying a special authorization from the Minister of the Navy and the Colonies."[27] Often omitted from the French national narrative, these facts show the difficulty in France, even under the Republic, in accepting equality between Black and white people. Contrary to a narrative that smooths over and neutralizes history, they also show the importance of race in the constitution of the nation. The restoration of slavery laid the foundations of an impossible equality.

The restoration of slavery in the colonies also meant the reaffirmation of white supremacy. Sent by Napoleon, Generals Richepanse and Gobert landed in Guadeloupe on May 28, 1802 with 4,000 men to implement the decree restoring slavery. Richepanse declared: "The title of French citizen throughout this island *will only be borne by Whites*. No other individual can claim this title, nor exercise the functions or employment that accompany it."[28] The colonies, he continued, were founded by whites, who were the "indigenous people of the French nation."[29] How much clearer need it be? In Saint-Domingue, Viscount de Rochambeau, who was hurried there by Napoleon to crush the insurrection, sent for dogs from Cuba, which he starved and sent raging mad before setting them on the enslaved, to the sound of military music and the encouragements and applause of the crowd. Accounts describe the perverse particularities of a society that took revenge, its fear whipped up into fury.[30] Sumptuous balls were thrown one after another in which Pauline Bonaparte and her court rivalled in elegance with "Mulatto women," while the soldiers burned, pillaged, and raped. In the last days of the Saint-Domingue colony, money, intrigues, avidity, avarice, and the pursuit of pleasure and luxury dominated white colonial society. Dessaline described the French soldiers as "blood-thirsty tigers." In his 1814 *Manifesto*, Henry Christophe, or Henry I, King of Haiti, described "the gallows erected everywhere, the drownings, the burnings at the stake, the most horrible tortures [that] were executed on his orders." The victory of the enslaved ended this tropical replica of the Ancien Régime. Over 10,000 planters left the island; they would fuel the fear of slave revolts, regularly brandishing the thread of another Haiti, and publishing reports portraying the Haitian Revolution as a bloody and barbaric uprising. Why recall these facts here? Because they belong to the history of State politics of protection, their racialization, and their sexism, for they notably explain the racist taboo in France of constituting community that does not obey the racial/national norms.

Forbidding community-building

Reproduction, Arlette Gautier writes, did not guarantee the improvement of a Black woman's lot.[31] On the plantations of Saint-Domingue:

> women's work and malnutrition had terrible repercussions on their fertility. Yet, in the last third of the eighteenth century, before the rapid rise in the price of slaves transported from Africa, and contrary to past decades when people preferred buying slaves, the trend on the big sugar plantations was, rather, to a push for as many children as

possible per female slave. Pregnancy was always tricky: miscarriages, abortions, and infanticides were common. While written sources do not in any way indicate whether these practices declined or increased over the years, the measures taken to prevent and punish them appear to have been increasingly frequent.[32]

According to a report written by the governor of Martinique, in 1763, colonizers made women work right up until the very end of their pregnancies, beat them because they were too slow, and sent them back to work immediately after giving birth, letting the new-born perish.[33] In 1838, although they could no longer depend on the trans-Atlantic trade, the island's planters opposed a project to introduce leave for pregnant women and women having recently given birth, as it would infringe their property rights. The slaveholders denied any difference between enslaved women and men, and instrumentalized them. Also subjected to sexual exploitation as breeders, men were allowed to occupy technical positions or positions of command on the plantation; women were responsible for care, cooking, reproduction and were the objects of sexual exploitation. Suffering from the lack of sexual differentiation of labor, the enslaved sought to recreate it outside the slaveholders' world.[34] Thanks to slave accounts or to longitudinal studies, North American and Brazilian historians have shown "that the slaves accorded great significance to their families and made huge efforts to maintain family ties despite being separated during slavery, and to find one another again after abolition."[35] Aware of both the lack of protection afforded by the plantation system, and the desire to thwart any community-based strategy and practice of protection, Black women and men developed their own systems of protection on all levels.

Violence against enslaved women was not just an unfortunate episode of an unfortunate history, nor the only example of colonial violence. Ignoring it perpetuates the illusion that the history of racialization under slavery was disconnected from this gender-based violence—especially as abolitionism did not seek to end it. The French abolitionist doctrine gave post-slavery colonial conquest a moral justification; it allegedly aimed to save populations subjugated by feudal and enslaving monarchies (as the French claimed in Madagascar), subjected to Oriental despotism (as they claimed in Algeria), or who were simply barbaric (as they claimed in Sub-Saharan Africa).[36] Right from its very creation, the Provisional Government of 1848, which announced the abolition of slavery in the French colonies on April 27, 1848, proclaimed that Algeria was now constitutionally an integral part of France. From 1842 to 1848, the Institut de l'Afrique, to which abolitionists belonged, advocated the colonization of the continent and the abolition of slavery and the trans-Atlantic slave trade in an effort to regenerate African populations. In May 1846, before the *Société française pour l'abolition de l'esclavage* (French Society for the Abolition of Slavery), of which he was one of the founders, Victor Schoelcher in person proposed to launch a petition for the freeing of slaves in Algeria, even though France had already embarked on the colonial conquest of this country.[37] Muslims became the figure of quintessential barbarians, the polar opposite of civilized—and thus abolitionist—Europeans.[38] From the Comoros to Zanzibar and Madagascar, the former slave-trading hubs in the Indian Ocean, slaves captured in Africa were sold as "free enlistees" and sent to the Americas or to the colonies in the Indian Ocean. In the slave colonies reigned a regime in which slaveholders behaved as sadistic, violent, and tyrannical patriarchs. For republican colonization to take place, this negative figure had to be erased and supplanted by that of the republican patriarch—strict, but benevolent—and that of the benevolent mother country. In Réunion, this process was captured in the following *Réunion Creole proverb*: *La sène fini kasé, ʒesclav touʒour amaré*, "The slave's chains are broken, but the slaves are still enchained."

In this breaking of community, let us not forget the disallowing of childhood. Sociological and psychological studies have repeatedly shown the differences to which urban and rural working-class girls and boys are daily subjected and their different treatment to bourgeois children.[39] Studies of racialized childhoods are less common. Few concepts define this condition in which the State denies children their right to childhood. While there is now growing knowledge of Indigenous children having been torn from their families and shut in residential schools in Canada, the United States, and Australia, even if its significance remains underestimated, that of the racially based denial of childhood in France is less common. The Palestinian criminology and law professor Nadera Shalhoub-Kevorkian proposes the concept of *unchilding* to describe the State politics that deny children the right to be children.[40] This denial reveals, on the part of the State, a differential administering of the protection of childhood according to race, class, age, and gender. The disallowing of childhood, of "being a community," are emanations of systemic and racial State violence, of which there is no lack of examples. One may cite the "Creuse children," the 2,150 children from Réunion torn from their parents and families between 1963 and 1982 to be adopted and serve as free labor on farms or as maids.[41] Or again, Zyed Benna and Bouna Traoré, respectively 17 and 15 years old, who were electrocuted on October 27, 2005 in Clichy-sous-Bois, and the ten years of legal proceedings, which closed in May 2015 following the acquittal of the two policemen charged with "failure to provide assistance to persons in peril." Adel Benna, Zyed's brother, declared at the time: "France has become a nightmare. Islamophobia and racism just keep on rising."[42] He added: "We can make our peace with Zyed's death, because we believe in destiny. But the persisting injustice; it's his memory they're defiling."[43] Two youths barely out of childhood but whose killing was not mourned by the whole country. They, it would appear, did not deserve to be called children; their panic during the chase by adult policemen, their distress, fear, and terror as they hid in an electrical substation and died was not seen to belong to stories of persecuted and brutalized childhoods. On this point, one may also evoke the bone tests used to determine whether a migrant is a minor or an adult. Yet these tests, which are based on statistical data collected between 1935 and 1941 from wealthy-class North American children and in which there is a significant margin of error, are not reliable. "A 14-year-old adolescent may have the bone maturity of an adult," lawyer Isabelle Zribi declared.[44] In the same vein, mention must be made too of youth detention centers, where isolation leads to suicide and self-harming, or the case of street children. The children in refugee camps in Greece, Syria, France, Bangladesh who commit suicide, have no access to schooling, and who are the object of sexual violence also come to mind.

While protection laws and laws criminalizing offenses against minors multiply, there are children who have no right to protection. Following Jamaican philosopher Sylvia Wynter's observation, according to whom we are still living in the fictional representation forged in the sixteenth century transforming the human into Universal Man (that is, white and Christian), we could say that childhood is a fiction created in Europe over the centuries, one which takes as its measure a white, male, bourgeois child.[45] This child—a boy, if he is well born—can be assured of the protection of the nation; a girl will necessarily come under scrutiny on several criteria, but State feminism has fought for her rights to be recognized.

My position, which insists on the need for racialized people to form communities, differs in that respect from Donna

Haraway's, for whom "Kin-making is making persons, not necessarily as individuals or as humans," but as elements of a whole, animals, plants, animate and inanimate matter included.[46] I understand what she means when she writes that "blaming Capitalism, Imperialism, Neoliberalism, Modernization, or some other 'not us' for ongoing destruction ... will not work either,"[47] but I cannot overlook the fact that not everybody has the same right to kin-making. Of course, in her call to create new forms of kin, she cites the "non-natalist kinnovations to individuals and collectives in queer, decolonial, and Indigenous worlds," which are more interesting than those of "European, Euro-American, Chinese, or Indian rich and wealth-extracting sectors." However, she overlooks the racial history of the forbidding of kinship. Applied to societies of the Global South, the ideology of "populationism" postulates that population is the main cause of social, political, and ecological problems.[48] Population control is thus envisaged as a coercive and at times violent fertility reduction politics more often than not targeting poor women of color, particularly in the Global South, but also in the North. For Ian Angus and Simon Butler, populationism produces a wider ensemble of processes that constrain bodies, families, and communities, producing segmented and segregated spaces, and determining which lives are precious and reproduceable, and which are not.[49]

It is not surprising that major powerful foundations invest in women of the South's contraception. Kalpana Wilson recalls that during the 2012 London Summit on Family Planning, the Bill & Melinda Gates Foundation and its partners, the United States Agency for International Development (USAID), the Department for International Development (DfID), the United Nations Population Fund (UNFPA), the pharmaceutical company Pfizer, and the American NGO Program for Appropriate Technology in Health (PATH), announced a new collaboration that aimed to "reach" three million women in sub-Saharan African and South Asia with 12 million doses of the Depo-Provera contraceptive within three years.[50] Another example was the DfID initiative in partnership with Merck to promote the contraceptive implant Implanon to "14.5 million of the poorest women" by 2015.[51] The deaths of 13 women who underwent surgical operations in the Chhattisgarh sterilization camps (India) in November 2014 is just one example among others of the atrocities and experiments perpetrated on poor and marginalized women.[52] "Far from giving poor women in the global South much-needed access to safe contraception which they can control, these policies dehumanize them as 'excessively reproductive' and set 'targets' which make atrocities like those of Chhattisgarh possible."[53]

Contemporary population control policies remain rooted in profoundly imperialist, racist, and patriarchal thinking. For the women and girls of the South, the experimentation with contraceptives and sterilization methods that are extremely dangerous for their health represents a highly lucrative market. Indeed, the world contraceptive market has risen from $11.2 billion in 2008 to $14.5 billion in 2016, and investments in the countries of the South have increased significantly.

3

The Impasse of
Punitive Feminism

"Fear must change sides"

"How many rapists must we kill before men stop raping women?", Egyptian feminist Mona Eltahawy asked in an Australian television interview on December 27, 2019.[1] The fact that the retransmission of this episode got censored was the proof, in Eltahawy's eyes, that the State only accepts condemnation of rape if it can set the terms and framework in which this condemnation is formulated and even determine the outcome. A woman can kill in self-defense and be pardoned by society and the State if she embodies the figure of the complete victim. Philosopher Elsa Dorlin develops a completely different politics of defense in her book, *Se défendre* (*Self-Defence: A philosophy of violence*). For feminists, the passage to violence, she writes, is "the logical consequence of an analysis of women's oppression and their minoritization as a structural feature of the State."[2] Why would women turn to the State to defend them, "considering that it is precisely the one who arms those who batter us."[3] The license to kill having been historically constituted, self-defense is a "process of rehumanization," writes Dorlin.[4] It is by overcoming the fear imposed by centuries of oppression, murder, torture, silencing through constantly readapted techniques that fear can change sides—in other words, by organizing self-defense.

The civility and the respectability advocated by white and bourgeois feminists do not provide the necessary force and energy to combat domination and oppression. On the contrary, they enable violence, says Eltahawy, proving themselves to be at the service of patriarchy and white supremacy. In refusing to be "polite," "nice," or "respectable," feminists uncover the hidden violence that demands respectability, and which can be summarized as follows: "you are authorized to speak if you respect patriarchal laws." With her "Fuck you feminism," Mona Eltahawy invites us to look patriarchy in the eye and to tell it: "I'm going to fucking destroy you."[5] The women of the Global South are caught between a rock and a hard place, Eltahawy continues. The rock is the racism and misogyny of the West, which, although untroubled by misogyny and patriarchy, claims to want to save the women who live "elsewhere"—the elsewhere that is neither Western nor white. The hard place is our communities, who want women to remain silent as speaking out can harm them. This critique of the choice between two patriarchies, two forms of sexism, in the name of the struggle's priorities has long been discussed by Black feminists and feminists of color. Aware that these two patriarchies and forms of sexism are not symmetric in the face of white power, that racialized men are the target of the violence of white supremacy and its feminist accomplices, they defend a theory and a praxis that aims to bring about a depatriarchalized, post-racial, and post-capitalist society. In this respect, making fear change sides becomes a political project.

Having witnessed the violence of the State, as it banned public meetings and demonstrations, having witnessed the violence of private militias armed by Réunion's big white landowners, who threatened anti-colonial activists with rape or death, I quickly understood that the public space is not neutral. The courage of the working classes as they confronted riot police and armed militias to free this space showed me that the State never exerts a complete monopoly over the public space. But even though I was encouraged to be curious about the world, I learned to remain vigilant on deserted station platforms after dark; I bought whistles; I learned to spot from afar the open and lit places—cafés, restaurants, shops—when coming home late at night; I learned to grip a key between two fingers and to aim for the neck; I took judo lessons; I learned not to catch someone's eye, or on the contrary to do so, to barricade doors and windows, to walk down empty corridors with assurance; I waited for my women friends to safely enter their houses, their doors shut, before pulling off; I spent money I did not have on taxis to get home from parties; the year that I lodged in dirt cheap Southern Californian motels frequented by marines out partying, I got into the habit of shoving a piece of furniture against my door and never opening it. And I more than once dreamed of acquiring tremendous physical strength and spent hours imagining scenarios to avenge humiliation or abuse to make fear change sides—a scenario that would give me a certain satisfaction.

Naomi Alderman's 2016 novel *The Power* tells the story of a radical reversal of this kind: all over the world, women discover that they have a power—the power to release deadly electrical jolts from their fingers—and they use it to defend themselves or to avenge abuse by men (confinement, denial of rights, sexual abuse, rape).[6] They gain this power after scientific military experimentation causes the massive pollution of rivers and water sources—in other words, men are punished for their own actions. It is a scenario in which the abuse of power leads to a power reversal, then. But the novel ends with women instituting punitive religions, creating armies that behave like imperialist forces, and turning men into a category to exploit and enslave. While the start of *The Power* can be read as an "empowerment fable," which "attempts to produce a powerful subjectivity to counter victimizing representations,"[7] it is the power to inflict death that allows the reversal. We need to be more imaginative, then; we need to overcome fear without resorting to fear and terror, while also overcoming domination.

Agnès Giard reminds us that fear has been

collectively constructed as a female trait. In other words, a woman, a real woman, must be afraid so that her way of investing public space is distinguished from that of men. Being afraid, women have to elaborate avoidance strategies. Wear headphones. Pretend to be talking on their cell phones. Avert their eyes, avoid sexy clothing. Sometimes, even, women must exclude themselves from certain spaces. Not that street. Not that neighborhood. Not at that time. Beware all contraveners, who get called to order: "I want your ass," "D'you fuck?," "You're hot." They are intimidated. They must be scared. Parents are the first to inculcate their daughters with the sentiment that their presence is 'illegitimate' after certain hours and in certain places. Surpassing these spatial boundaries is to expose oneself to the risk of violence.[8]

Even though studies show that violence is above all inflicted in the private sphere (it is this space that represents a mortal danger for women), it is the public space that is perceived as the most dangerous.[9] For Valérie Rey-Robert, author of *Une culture du viol à la française* (*French Rape Culture*), "women report being afraid in two types of spaces in particular: large and often deserted open spaces, such as parks, woods, forests, wastelands, or the countryside, and closed spaces with few exits where men can hide and attack women without them being able to escape."[10] Urban architecture was not conceived to encourage a peaceful social life; it is hostile to women, and in particular to racialized women, homeless people, refugees, the elderly, migrants, poor people, disabled people, Black people, Arabs. Towns are structured to prevent their circulation; they contain "invisible walls" that racialized people, women, children must learn to identify in order to circumvent and avoid them. For geographer Yves Raibaud, public policies obey both "normative masculine codes" and social and racial ones.[11] The violence that urban architecture normalizes, naturalizes, cannot be abolished by escalating militarized police presence and surveillance. Towns, which have been turned into hostile and inhospitable bourgeois settlements, need to be reappropriated by those who have historically been excluded from them.

Desire for revenge, thirst for punishment

All over the world, women are disproportionately affected by systemic, gender-based and sexual violence, by the lack of access to land, by discrimination and exploitation in the labor market. Every day in the world, on average, 137 women are killed by a man known to them, over a third by a current or ex-husband or partner.[12] Globally, approximately 15 million teenage girls aged 15 to 19 have been subjected to forced sexual intercourse (penetration or other forcibly imposed sexual acts) at some point in their lives.[13] According to UN-Women, 30 percent of women in the world aged 15 and over "have been subjected to intimate partner violence, non-partner sexual violence, or both at least once in their life … This figure does not include sexual harassment."[14] Transgender people and people who do not identify with a given gender are more frequently targeted by violence. However, as not all assaults against cisgender, transgender, non-binary, and lesbian women throughout the world every year are registered, and as non-white women are underrepresented in these figures because the violence committed against them and their murder are considered to matter less, race, class, gender, and sexual discriminations need to be included in these estimations to give a full picture of the systemic violence against women. In South Africa, a woman is killed every three hours,[15] 150 women are raped every day, and lesbians are victims of so-called "corrective rape" meant to "cure" them.[16] In Spain, after the rape and murder of 19 women by a current or former partner in the summer of 2019 alone, feminist movements declared a state of emergency.[17] In Argentina, during the first six months of 2019, 155 femicides were recorded, six of which targeted trans women; the majority of the victims were 18 years old or less.[18] In Brazil, "Black women are often seen as sexual objects ... In the rural world, they are often the first victims of violence, including sexual violence."[19] In France every year, 220,000 adult women are victim to physical and/or sexual violence inflicted by their current or ex-partners, and 43 percent of French women declare they have been subjected to non-consensual sexual acts.[20] Every day, women who wear the hijab are discriminated against and met with opprobrium. In the United States, Black women are assassinated at a higher rate than all other categories of women,[21] and Indigenous women are the most vulnerablized, provoking a very high rate of suicide among them.[22] One in three American women live on or below the poverty line, and in New York City, the rate of Black women who die in childbirth is twelve times higher than it is for white women.[23] Racialized girls and boys aged 12 to 14 run the highest risk of being raped and being the victim of an aggression.[24] In Canada, Indigenous women's groups estimate that the number of Indigenous women assassinated or gone missing at over 4,000, and this, for decades, to the utmost indifference of the police.[25] In India in 2019, four rapes occurred per hour.[26] In 2012, the gang rape and murder of a student on a bus in Delhi sparked a large protest movement, which the BJP government responded to by proposing to introduce the death penalty for rapists. Violence against women was met with State violence against men, especially if they were Dalit, as shown by the Indian police's assassination of four suspects in the gang rape of a young 27-year-old woman.[27] In the national Parliament, the BJP woman MP Jaya Bachchan considered that the guilty should be "publicly lynched," and one of her male colleagues demanded, in addition to a register of sex offenders, that rapists be castrated.[28] The lawyer and activist Vrinda Grover has denounced this "arbitrary violence," and notably that of the Indian police, often accused of carrying out extra-judicial murders to cover up badly handled investigations or to calm public opinion: "The police must be accountable. Instead of carrying out an investigation and gathering proof, the State commits murders to satisfy the public and to avoid having to be accountable."[29] Statistics also show that depression rates among female victims of physical or sexual violence inflicted by their partners are higher than for women who have not suffered these forms of violence.[30] Added to this systemic violence is the violence of organized poverty and fabricated vulnerability.[31] These figures say nothing of singular lives and their complexity; they reduce lived experiences to percentages, erase responses and struggles, but their amplitude explains the rage that seizes us on their enumeration.

The desire for revenge and punishment is, as a result, completely understandable. Imagining a reversal of roles, cornering a man to humiliate him, to make him concretely, physically realize what a woman upon whom a man imposes his violence feels is completely understandable. Once violence is associated with a community of men considered to all be the same and to all be united in their hatred of women and their desire to humiliate them, to harm them, to torture and to kill them, the desire for repression is almost spontaneous.

Has not this violence always existed? In all cultures? Are not men structurally violent and women always their victims? Are not laws too lenient given that violence is not decreasing, or hardly? Let's pillory men! Banish them! Take away their parenting rights! Let them discover what it is to feel fear, terror, to panic, then to continue to feel terrorized, weak, a victim! Let them be the target of our rage! Lock them up! Let fear change sides! But if all the forms of punishment, the death penalty, lynching, the ever-longer prison sentences, the impossible re-integration into society do not ensure the end of violence against women, if, although constrained for a moment, it resurfaces with force and cruelty, what measures will make fear change sides? What incites men to kill? Why are not women better protected? Why, according to a study in France, is it exes who in the majority kill the women who have left them? Why can't men stand being abandoned when they have no apparent difficulty in abandoning?

The African-American science-fiction author Octavia Butler proposes another scenario to that of mirroring violence to combat violence: that of *miraculous weapons*. Through this prism, the peaceful and the imaginative are able to save the humanity of an apocalyptic world. In her "Parable series," her heroine Olamina is afflicted with a "hyper empathy" syndrome: she feels others' pleasure and pain one hundredfold. In a State ravaged by civil wars and governed by a fundamentalist Christian who wants to Make America Great Again, Olamina uses her syndrome to lead the resistance. "My heroine is a fighter," Octavia Butler explained in one interview:[32]

I had to work really hard to make her a people's leader as it is not in my nature. I find people who seek power suspect. I did everything for my heroine to be a leader: she is the eldest of a family of five children, the other four of whom are brothers. She is also the daughter of the original community leader and the daughter-in-law of the only teacher in the neighborhood ... She was born to take on responsibility.[33]

Head of the resistance, Olamina reinvents what constitutes family and creates a community to "rescue and ... redefine humanity."[34] The Black heroines imagined by Octavia Butler are not "ultimate universal subjects," but women who seek to survive and to help their kin survive in a hostile society. Andrea Hairston writes:

Butler's characters value community over individual success. Or better, individual success is defined in terms of community. Her questions are: what do we do to survive? How must we change if we are not to be wiped out by others, by ourselves? Her stories focus on those who make the compromises, those who do not have the power to determine their place in society, those who are forced to lives defined by more powerful beings/forces.[35]

As Angelyn Mitchell remarks, by taking the view of those with the least power and who are the most brutalized, Butler describes the considerable effort it takes, and the difficulties encountered, to preserve dignity, humanity, and community in a world that structurally negates them.[36] By recognizing the existence of the hurdles and the painful decisions that confront oppressed women throughout the world to ensure their survival, and that of their children and their communities, Butler surpasses the ideology of punishment and all-out carcerality.

Ending the penal system: the impasses of carceral feminism

Based on notions of dangerousness and security, carceral feminism is an ideology that calls for courts to judge more severely and to hand down longer prison sentences, or for an increase in measures of surveillance and control.[37] For Elizabeth Bernstein, neoliberalism marked a decisive turning point for movements with feminist agendas, previously organized around struggles for freedom and economic justice.[38] In this lineage, carceral feminism "seeks social remedies through criminal justice interventions rather than through a redistributive welfare state, and ... advocates for the beneficence of the privileged rather than the empowerment of the oppressed."[39] Rather than fighting for the advent of feminist liberation, the "carceral turn" has reduced feminism to the individual and the punitive, and marginalized the collective and redistributive.[40]

Is the criminal system the best placed to bring justice in the case of violence against women? Is it capable of protecting women from violence and abuse? All these questions point to profound divisions among feminists, echoing different ideological approaches to the State and the penal system. Indeed, what common ground is there between these two affirmations: "the carceral conditions of men found guilty of committing an aggression against women are unacceptable, for they entail dehumanization, objectification, and invisibilization," and "how to provide safety to a female victim of domestic violence, who might potentially be in danger of death, other than by locking up her partner?"[41] How to reconcile such a disparity between "it is not imprisoning an aggressor that will change his mentality and teach him that a woman is a human being,"[42] and "taking legal action appears irremediable"?[43] This division seems to me particularly fecund, as it once again shows the existence of *several* feminisms. One current among so many others seeks State and penal backing to bring about a more peaceful society. We do not need to deplore it, but simply to analyze and fight it. There are enough women's struggles that do not adopt this bent, thereby precisely justifying the existence of anti-carceral liberation feminisms.

Prisons will not save us from patriarchy or violence

Prison, Gwenola Ricordeau writes, "constitutes a blind spot for contemporary feminist movements, with the notable exception of the unjust condemnations meted out to women victims of violence."[44] The history of relations between French feminists and the criminal justice system and prison is in fact a little more complex. There is no consensus in European and French feminist movements. In the second half of the twentieth century, women denounced the colonial justice system and the prison conditions in which anti-colonial activists were held. Prison was described as one of the structures of colonialism and racism, and the justice system as an auxiliary of colonial power. In France in the 1970s, governments met contestation and strikes with increased repression and imprisonment. The term *sécuritaire* ("law and order") emerged and replaced "security." Prison became one of the sites of the struggle against the State and its criminal justice system. The distinction between political prisoners and common-law prisoners was challenged, as both were prisoners of the State. The only difference between activists accused of jeopardizing State security and ordinary offenders was their stated intentions; both were the victims of the same system of repression and impoverishment. Hunger strikes, which the collective movement of Algerian detainees in French prisons had used as a weapon in the late 1950s, inspired political prisoners in the 1970s.[45] Thirty-nine detainees, including twelve women, all of whom were Maoist militants, went on hunger strike in 1970.[46] They demanded that the "special detention regime" be granted to those among them not already benefitting from it, and the improvement of the modalities of the application of this "special regime". One of the detainees, Marc Hatzfeld, addressed an open letter to the governor of the Santé Prison in Paris:

We would like to state that we consider common-law prisoners to be the product of a society, police, and a carceral system that traps them in their condition of "delinquents". We are here precisely because we are fighting against this society. Furthermore, we consider that the reaction that drives these "delinquents" to individual acts—that we do not judge in themselves—stems more often than not from a revolt whose nature is eminently political. If we have taken the decision to not remain passive today, it is thus precisely out of solidarity with the entire prison population and so that it, in its entirety, can benefit from our action.

[On September 15,] around thirty wives and mothers of hunger-striking detainees demonstrated [to protest against the detainees' prison conditions] in front of the Ministry of Justice and demanded the "special regime." The women were not given an audience. They attempted to unfurl a banner that was torn down by plain-clothes policemen, and bore banners inscribed, "Down with prisons!", "Political regime!" They were also confiscated by the police.[47]

In October of the same year, women from the MLF (Women's Liberation Movement) held a demonstration in front of the Petite Roquette women's prison in central Paris, constructed as a panopticon (that is, allowing a single guard positioned in a central tower to keep watch over all the prisoners at the same time), where female Algerian nationalist militants and the French women who supported their struggle had been locked up:[48]

One October evening, that oh so symbolic month.[49] A disturbance. [Cathy Bernheim] handed out tracts on the sidewalk while some forty women marched in the street, tied together with meters of chains that they had wrapped around their wrists, shouting very loud so that the inmates could hear them. They publicly claimed for the first time that the women prisoners were the political prisoners of a specific power: the patriarchy. That the women incarcerated for prostitution, abortion, fraud, or even crimes were the sisters of those shouting outside their windows.[50]

Political groups and intellectuals (only men headed the committees) mobilized against the prison. On January 27, 1971, several hundred Maoist activists from the "27 May Movement" gathered in front of the Petite Roquette shouting: "Down with prisons! Freedom!," "Pleven, scum! The people will have your hide!"[51] Testimonies about France's women's prisons are rare. There are of course those of the Algerian women combatants, then, in 1965, in the novel *L'Astragale* by Albertine Sarrazin, but women detainees have largely remained invisible. In February 1971, the anonymous testimony of a political detainee at the Petite Roquette prison revealed the living conditions and social hierarchy of a women's prison. Guarded by nuns, as under the Ancien Régime (late sixteenth to late eighteenth century), the poorest prisoners were exploited for dirt wages:

From nine to eleven thirty in the morning, work in the workshop, under the surveillance of a nun. For fifty centimes an hour, [the fashion brands] D. Hechter, Christian Dior, Cardin, and the SNCF [the French national railway company] find a totally exploitable workforce, that no minimum wage will ever protect. Some particularly impoverished prisoners have been condemned by the judge to carry out the hardest labor: jailers assigned [them] the heaviest burdens, getting up an hour earlier; washerwomen working the heavy machines in the stinking atmosphere of the laundry room. Others have been given less exhausting work: accounting, the library. The detainees with no money have to work as in prison, everything must be bought, via the canteen, from writing paper to cigarettes, to knitting needles, shampoo, packets of sanitary towels, and packets of biscuits. All those who are already condemned have to work in the workshop or the prison. For abortionists, drug addicts, madams, and political detainees, special treatment: complete solitary confinement.[52]

On February 8, 1971, during a press conference at the Saint-Bernard chapel in Paris, philosopher Michel Foucault announced the creation of the *Groupe d'information sur les prisons* (Prison Information Group, or GIP), whose mission was to inform people about daily life in prison. The GIP manifesto began as follows:

No one can be certain that they will never go to prison. Today less than ever. Police control of our daily lives is getting tighter: in the streets and on the roads; of foreigners and young people; the crime of opinion has resurfaced; anti-drug measures are exacerbating arbitrariness. We are under the sign of "detention." We are told that the justice system is overrun, which we can well see. But what if it were the police who had overrun it? We are told that the prisons are overpopulated. But what if it were the population that was over-incarcerated?[53]

Prison remained a depot in which to cram the bodies designated dangerous, the riff-raff, the wretched, the poor, the beggars, the destitute, a depot in which to lock up all who, by their very presence, might question the period's narrative of a society of performing winners. Mutinies broke out in several men's prisons in 1971. They were severely repressed. At government level, they opened the door to a policy of "humanitarian" prisons.

In 1975, in his book *Discipline and Punish*, Michel Foucault revealed the ways in which prison is indispensable to the functioning of the State and how it impresses on society the notion that, to protect that society, it is necessary to lock away and punish people. The notion of dangerousness, he wrote, helps reinforce a feeling of insecurity, which in turn justifies an ideology of law and order, which then exacerbates the perception of danger. This notion has endurably marked the State and security-based ideology of protection, and is behind a whole host of repressive laws, this feeling of insecurity being "inversely proportional to real insecurity."[54] That same year, several groups within the MLF mobilized against the torture and incarceration of Basque women by Franco's dictatorship and denounced the connections between fascism, violence, the torture of women, and the carceral system. The imprisonment of women was seen as one of the arms of the fascist State and of the patriarchal State. It can thus be asserted that, in the 1970s in France, as in the rest of the world, prison was a terrain of political combat—notably from the feminists' point of view. I shall later discuss the abolitionist current in the United States, which advocates the abolition of prisons.

The 1970s saw the emergence of a discourse of law and order and the emergence in the media of figures identified with insecurity and delinquency: young, poor, foreign, immigrant, descendants of post-colonial immigrant men, living in the *cité*, or housing projects. Studies of these law-and-order discourses and their representations illustrate their progressive racialization and ethnicization. On February 18, 1976, Roger Gicquel opened the main television station's evening newsflash, stating: "France is scared."[55] In the 1980s, insecurity became an "array of solutions thought up to mask the most visible effects of the disorganization and demoralization of working-class milieux."[56] Violence was detached from its economic and social context, and even though society was "on the whole less violent than in the past," the feeling of insecurity and powerlessness rose. For the sociologist Laurent Muchielli, it was "the evolution of values, the increasing wealth gap, the ways of living in towns and villages, family tragedies, school drop-out rates, the extent of unemployment, and the ghettoization of certain neighborhoods" that were at play in the production of this feeling of insecurity.[57]

In the women's groups that constituted the MLF, appeals to the criminal justice system provoked heated debates. While in 1977, during a colloquium on "Women and Violence," members of the Spectacular Violences group went as far as proposing to "train female commandos who would beat up guys chosen randomly ... or maybe for how they looked, saying to them: 'You look like you want to rape' exactly in the same way as they tell us 'you look like you want to be raped,'"[58] the debate above all focused on the pertinence of turning to the criminal justice system. Although they diverged on several points, the women who wrote in *Femmes travailleuses en lutte*, *Les Cahiers du féminisme*, *Le Quotidien des femmes*, *Le torchon brûle*, *Histoires d'elles*, and *Les Cahiers du GRIF* shared the same mistrust of the criminal justice system. To turn to the law, to the justice system, was to admit the collective failure of the MLF, as repressive laws only "reinforced and upheld rape and violence."[59] Several feminists—lawyers, activists, etc.—expressed their refusal or their discomfort before "the legalist illusion," the judicial institution being "the terrain of the adversary par excellence," wrote lawyer Odile Dhavernas.[60] Following the first major rape trial in 1978 where the feminist lawyer Gisèle Halimi defended two women accusing a group of men of rape, a trial which mobilized severral groups of the Women's Liberation Movement, the feminist and founder of the *Front homosexuel d'action révolutionnaire* (Homosexual Front for Revolutionary Action)[61] Françoise d'Eaubonne recounted that she contacted men and women inmates at Fresnes prison. These prisoners, and the partners of prisoners with whom she corresponded told her: "there is no valid reason to increase the herd of incarcerated; there is no law, however harsh, that prevents the phenomenon of 'rape'—on the contrary, even."[62] This argument was strongly contested by some feminists: "We don't care about class justice. We have (in the name of the struggle of the same name) been sidetracked enough from our immediate and probing concerns."[63] As regards the criminal justice system, positions seemed irreconcilable. On the one hand was the position that declared: "the difficulty in reconciling our position (that we are not asking for repression) and that of women who to all intents and purpose demand it because they are afraid very quickly emerged."[64] On the other was the position which claimed that a law against violence would "fundamentally change nothing for women," as it would be based on "the imposture which consists in pretending that respect for women will be measured in the number of years behind bars handed down in trials."[65] Gisèle Halimi,[66] for her part, adopted the in-between position, stating: "Whatever the crime, all long-term prison sentences are individually destructive, detrimental, and socially pointless," yet added, "it is nonetheless unacceptable that rape sentences alone, and in priority, be abolished or reduced."[67] Feminists had, of course, to "confront the repressive logic of this (judicial) machine, its carceral system and, above all, its virulent misogyny," but, they wrote, the "problem of repression cannot be ours as a priority: it is the defense of rape victims that interests our feminist combat. And it is indeed certain that, on this question, our struggle must be constantly reformulated."[68]

In Europe, these debates were not limited to France. In Italy, during the debate about a draft law to counter violence against women backed by feminists and the Italian left,[69] feminists from the Milan Women's Bookstore Collective judged it "unacceptable" that "in the name of all, a handful of women [handed over] this specific suffering [of violence against women] to the interventions and tutelage of the State."[70] The draft law, which favored a "top-down, expeditious solution from the outside," turned women into an "oppressed and thus homogeneous social group and the object of tutelage," "again and always crushed in a paralyzing dependency and state of destitution," to force them "to progress, and thus to enter the courtroom to defend female dignity."[71] Yet, the law is not neutral; it is the emanation of the patriarchal and capitalist State. Distance "from the law of the father which regulates sexuality and symbolization" is necessary.[72] "The idea of resolving the contradiction between the sexes through the law" was a red herring.[73] The struggle was turned "into a procedure, and consciousness raising into a banal normative registering."[74] The Milan feminists posed the following questions: "Do we really want to transition from personal authority to public authority? Do we really want to transition from the marginality of our official quasi-inexistence to a citizen's existence equal to that of men?"[75] This marginality, they claimed, was not a weakness; it was the basis of an alternative project, for women could not trust a political representation that, even when undertaken by women, reduced women to silence.

While, in the light of these elements, it is thus possible to qualify Gwenola Ricordeau's remark about French feminism's indifference to the criminal justice system and prisons, questions nonetheless remain: why did no organized abolitionist feminist movement emerge from these mobilizations? Why have colonial prisons and those of the "Overseas Territories" never been included in the study of prisons? What are the connections between colonial justice/prison and post-colonial justice/prison? How to explain the marginalization of racialization and class in French mobilizations against gender-based and sexual violence? How did carceral feminism emerge? What role does the amnesia surrounding anti-colonial and anti-racist struggles play in these positions on the carceral question and in the evolution towards a civilizational, State, and femo-nationalist feminism?

Socialist femocrats: from whorephobia to the ideology of law and order

In June 1975, a group of prostitutes (that is what they called themselves, the term "sex worker" not yet having come into usage) decided to occupy a church in Lyon, France, with the following slogan: "Our children don't want their mothers going to prison."[76] They were protesting against a law that condemned passive soliciting re-offenders to prison. The feminists who supported them admitted that they did not always understand their position: "in a nutshell, they wanted to do their trade in fit conditions and we, even if we weren't able to say so, wanted to end this work."[77] In tracts handed out in Lyon, feminists drew a parallel between sex work and sexual harassment in the workplace and home: "Whether their boss or their husband, to keep their jobs and material security … it's not just on sidewalks that women end up prostituting themselves … Forced marriages put us in the same situation as prostitutes, obliged to sell our bodies and souls to our lord and master to survive and to gain a respectable place in this male society."[78] In the same way that European women had compared their situation to that of enslaved Black women in the eighteenth century, twentieth-century feminists compared their loss of autonomy in the workplace and home to the situation of sex workers. This temptation to draw analogies between situations that are only similar at face value has proven itself to be a constant of universalist feminism.

In the 1980s and 1990s, femocrats from the French Socialist Party and other feminists seized on the abolition of prostitution, providing the State with the vocabulary of carceral/punitive and moralist feminism, and influencing the content of repressive laws in the name of protecting women—prostitution becoming the symbol of their oppression. It was in the ranks of the French Socialist Party that a State carceral feminism emerged, writes Lilian Mathieu,[79] and it was in France that the first laws redefining public morals were adopted.[80] Historically, the question of prostitution has constituted a "rallying point for groups with diverging demands and interests, but whose common project is the assertion of women's social (and moral) role."[81] Attitudes towards sex work divided feminists. Even the word "work" was refuted.

While the ideological conflicts within feminism over prostitution do not correspond (directly) to a distinction between conservative and revolutionary politics, it is nonetheless important to recognize the role that French Socialist femocrats played in the law-and-order-based discourse of class and race. Abolishing prostitution became their battle cry. The abolition campaign, which was led in the 1980s by "abolitionist femocrats and abolitionists from the associative and militant field,"[82] and backed by Socialist ministers such as Lionel Jospin and Ségolène Royal, managed to forge a left-to-right consensus in the French National Assembly. Sex work became the quintessential site of new forms of the enslavement and oppression of women, who only a Western State and its police could save. The abolitionist lobby was bolstered "in the Socialist Party, State feminist bodies, and the associative field"[83] by the ideology of law and order. It was the most vulnerable who came to represent danger—male and female sex workers, trans people, poor people, racialized people—and laws were there to exclude them. In the name of women's protection, carceral feminism offered a vocabulary and an ideology in which dangerousness, the logics of law and order, crime, and criminality structured the entire discourse. Considering prostitution as "another form of rape," some parliamentarians demanded that "the buying of sexual services be considered not a simple infraction, but an offense, or even a crime."[84]

For its first major campaign, which prepared the terrain for the debate on the law "destined to reinforce the fight against the system of prostitution and to accompany prostituted people," French Socialist Party feminists made the "figure of the prostitute-victim—presented under the traits of a naïve, vulnerable, young foreign woman" a central image.[85] Prostitution was a threat to the entire society, and particularly to women: "The system of prostitution hurts women, all women. It symbolizes their subordination and their potential relegation to the status of sexual merchandise. And, like all other sexist discriminations, it is an obstacle to social, economic, and political equality."[86] "We are not afraid to say that it is above all on behalf of the undocumented, battered, humiliated foreign female minor that we need to act," declared the right-wing UMP parliamentarian Marie-Louise Fort.[87] As recently as 2016, the Socialist MP for Paris, Danièle Hoffman-Rispal, said: "We have abandoned the idea that these women are guilty too; no, they are victims."[88] Stories of trafficked and martyrized women contribute to the discourse of vulnerability that demands a humanitarian State intervention. The female sex worker is an *absolute* victim, naïve, foreign (which makes it possible to connect the abolition of prostitution to anti-migrant laws); her profession is detrimental to *all* women. The State must intervene to protect both foreign vulnerable women, and "its" women. For male and female sex workers, this politics "invisibilizes their rights, fuels puritanism, and imposes middle-class white European women's conservative conception of sex."[89] The members of the French sex workers' union, STRASS, denounce abolitionism in these terms: "Not pro-abolition, nor pro-regulation: pro-unions!", and fights "against the criminalization of sex work, for the application of common law to male and female sex workers."[90]

In 2002, the then Minister of the Interior in France, Nicolas Sarkozy, announced that the security law he was preparing would contain "dispositions authorizing the deportation of foreign prostitutes guilty of solicitation. Indeed, the offense of passive soliciting, removed from the criminal code in 1994, will be reintroduced, exposing those found guilty to prison sentences and steep fines."[91] Sarkozy's declaration caused male, female, cis, and trans sex workers to march in protest, marches that white feminists did not participate in, Lilian Mathieu recounts, because they "refused to join the prostitutes' mobilization as the latter voiced demands unacceptable to the feminists, such as the official recognition of prostitution as a 'profession,' and its spokespeople were considered illegitimate as they were strongly suspected of being manipulated by pimps."[92] The *Collectif national pour les droits des femmes* (National Collective for Women's Rights) demonstrated on December 10 on a triple call to action: "No to the system of prostitution, no to Sarkozy's draft bill, yes to a prostitution-free world."

The Security Law of March 2003, which, in the name of the protection of women, punished sex workers' passive soliciting with prison and fines, aimed to remove from the streets the presence of racialized female bodies that, with their clothing, "sullied" the public space. It also sought to remove from French soil the bodies of women of the Global South, whose work was "an insult" to women's rights.[93] The street had to be cleansed of these bodies so that white women—whom this presence inconvenienced and offended (the sexualization of bodies, the visibility of sex work)—could feel protected and free. Protection was expressed here in terms of indignation at the traffic of women from the Global South, perceived as the victims of Black and Arab traffickers, without questioning the reasons that drive these women to leave their countries in the hope of a wage, for that would have then required analyzing the entanglement of violence, imperialism, and capitalism, which necessarily invoke predatory sources of enrichment. The black or brown body is a merchandise trafficked from South to North; its vulnerability and precarity are the result "of the demands and requirements exported from the economic centers and major world powers and redistributed by globalization and the media."[94] In other words, the predatory commodification of bodies has nothing to do with so-called "civilizational backwardness"; it is perfectly integrated into the logics of capitalism. In this context, presented as a law to protect women, the 2003 bill was just one facet of a politics of protection whose goal was to reinforce the whitewashing of French towns and to justify the persecution and expulsion of racialized women in the name of women's rights. A whole host of laws and practices began to regulate the presence of racialized bodies in towns. There are women who are authorized to circulate in the streets on the condition that they remain invisible, discreet, effaced. They are the ones who clean the city, those to whom bourgeois families entrust their children and the keys of their domestic spaces, authorizing them to witness intimate scenes. Racialized young and adult men are authorized to enter the city on the condition that they do invisibilized but necessary jobs (shop, museum, gallery, shopping mall, theatre, and nightclub security guards), or jobs that are subaltern but necessary to urban life (couriers, deliverymen). Their circulation is actively surveilled and controlled, however. Other racialized people are not authorized to circulate freely in cities; they risk arrest and eviction. The laws that organize the circulation and presence of racialized people in towns racialize immiseration. Indeed, in recent years, we have witnessed the emergence of the neoliberal subject who offers State, universalist, and civilizational feminists a terrain they have rapidly seized upon. This neoliberal subject, which may even grant the racialized subject an ideological integration, finds the source of its archive in communication technologies, that is, a selection of dates, actions, and figures that erase all historicity and reserve the central place to the universalist feminist movement.[95]

In 2012, Najat Vallaud-Belkacem, the Socialist government's Minister of Women's Rights, continued to use the vocabulary of punitive feminism: "The question isn't whether we want to abolish prostitution—the answer is yes—but rather giving ourselves the means to do so. My objective, like that of the Socialist Party, is to see the end of prostitution."[96] The association *Osez le féminisme* (Dare Embrace Feminism) applauded: "we are delighted that she has rooted [her] mandate as Minister of Women's Rights in a [prostitution] abolitionist position. And, above all, we are delighted that she wants to translate this position into acts and facts."[97] Gabrielle Partenza, a prostitute "since 1969" who set up the association *Avec nos aînées* (With Our Elders) to help elder women out of prostitution, analyzed this declaration as follows:

> the discourse according to which prostitutes are poor girls who don't know what they are doing, who are the victims of their clients, must end. It shows real ignorance of the profession to say that! They want to abolish prostitution saying it's "for the good" of prostitutes. The abolition fundamentalists equate "traditional workers" with Eastern European girls, but there are free and independent prostitutes. Those who are in the hands of networks are slaves, not prostitutes. Free them, save those who don't want to enter into prostitution, ask yourselves what means you're going to put at their

disposal so they can stop doing a job they don't want to do, but the others, leave them the hell alone![98]

In her study of relations between prostitute and feminist movements from 1975 to 2020, Lilian Mathieu points out that most of the protagonists chose to overlook "that it was based on a draft bill—rarely mentioned in their exchanges—that granted the police additional repressive means to use against already particularly fragile and precarious populations, and displaying a logic of criminalizing poverty, that the debate on prostitution was born."[99] Carceral feminism "easily accommodated law and order and anti-immigration policies targeting (foreign) women and excluding them from the scope of women's rights."[100] For Miriam Ticktin, the fact of combining "violence, sexual violence, and the surveillance of families" lead to "a clear action: the closing of borders."[101] While, as Jacquemart and Jakšić point out, carceral feminism is not new, while it is only one expression of a feminism still hampered in its objectives by the very thing it seeks to serve (the State), it is important to better understand its role in the growing apparatus of surveillance and punishment.

Protecting public space, excluding racialized and poor people

An environment hostile to racialized and poor people constructs enemies who must be spotted, surveilled, and excluded from the public space. In the 1980s, women wearing hijabs in France were among such dangerous presences. For the ex-Socialist Minister of Women's Rights Yvette Roudy, "The burqa is a sign of organized domination. Women's identity is erased ... It's a downward spiral; we need a law."[102] In a tribune, feminists Anne Vigerie and Anne Zelensky, who saw the hijab as a threat to security and to women's rights, reversed the accusation of racism against the very people subjected to and denouncing it:

> In our scarcely assumed guilt-ridden post-colonial society, the phobia of being accused of racism by *"rejection of the other"* leads to an unreasoned sacralization of difference. We are thus living under the thumb of a political correctness inherited from *"left-wing"* reflexes, to which even the right is victim. This is how, in the name of respect for customs, we were shamed when we decided to denounce female genital mutilation and to bring to justice cases of FGM. Islamists unhesitatingly play extensively on this scared state of mind that takes refuge in a tolerance on all fronts ... In reality, the tragedy is that this kind of political correctness is a veritable racism blind to itself but which survives and reincarnates in the apparent anti-racism of the "right to difference." Islamist bigotry, whose Christian equivalent would outrage us, is "perfectly okay for Maghrebis."[103]

What has emerged over the past few decades is a reconfiguration of Orientalist discourse, which freezes women in alterity and forces them to exploit these Orientalist representations through which "I am this Other who needs saving."[104]

In France in the early 2000s, media campaigns into "hood gang rapes," and then "men-only cafés and neighborhoods," portrayed working-class districts as spaces hostile to white and racialized women, allegedly controlled by racialized men.[105] Samira Bellil's 2002 autobiographical account *To Hell and Back: The Life of Samira Bellil*, which denounced her gang rape, the silence imposed on her by her entourage, and the indifference of the justice system, triggered a media and political storm. My point here is not to question her account, but to consider what the media, commentators, and feminists did with it, and how social fear of working-class racialized neighborhoods and the stigmatization of their populations were reinforced. For the sociologist Laurent Mucchielli, the press, which gave this rape a "massive echo chamber," transformed "this individual story" into a "symbol of an entire country."[106] Housing projects became spaces inhabited by "wolf kids. Aged 10 to 15, they trash, steal, extort, kill even. They are known as 'the new barbarians'."[107] In 2006, Agence France Presse (AFP) made the parallel between gang rapes and an infamous pedophile criminal scandal in Outreau, France: "Gang rapes in Fontenay-sous-Bois: the inhabitants evoke the specter of Outreau."[108] The "gang rape scandal" revealed that "gang rape has sadly always existed in French society, as it has in others. Gang rapes appear neither to be new, nor on the increase over the last forty years or so. What is more, there is no evidence of a concentration in working-class milieux and so-called 'sensitive' neighborhoods."[109] In his study of this mediatization, Mucchielli highlights the amalgamation between gang rapes and Islam, and the fact that the acts of young men of Maghrebi origin, or black-skinned young men are over-mediatized compared to other events of the same nature when they take place in other areas of France, in wealthier neighborhoods, or in the rural milieu. As Claire Cosquer argues:

> gang rapes are the object of a moral narrative: journalists feign their astonishment at a radical form of amorality. The latter is presented as intrinsically *banlieusarde*, or characteristic of the *banlieue*,[110] thereby engaging a mechanism of extension, in the sense that the suspects and guilty parties are not presented as asocial beings incapable of understanding the moral principles that forbid rape, but, on the contrary, as excessively social, symbols of *banlieusarde* socialization, and trapped in a strict determinism.[111]

The housing projects become the antithesis of society, the former believed to be in collusion with criminals through their imposing silence on their victims, threatening them with retaliation, and protecting rapists, contrary to the latter, who want women to be free. With the *Ni putes ni soumises* (Neither Whores Nor Submissive) association, French civilizational feminism created an auxiliary force of racialized women who had all the attributes associated with the "Oriental woman," only with a modern twist, as they denounced their community's male chauvinism and adhered to the ideology of integration.

To give a more recent example of this type of moral panic, in 2016, Nadia Remadna rang the alarm: cafés in poor racialized neighborhoods were out of bounds to women.[112] Pascale Boistard, the former Socialist government's Secretary of State for Women's Rights, jumped on the bandwagon: "There are zones in our country where women are not allowed."[113] Sent to the *département* of Seine-Saint-Denis (93) in the Paris *banlieue* to investigate a café in Sevran identified as hostile to women's presence, women journalists from France Télévision reportedly heard: "You're in the 93 here, you aren't in Paris! It's a different mentality here, it's like being in the *bled*!"[114] In the report, which was broadcast at prime time, the voice-over explained this state of affairs: "Why do the men reject women? It's a problem of tradition, culture, but also religion."[115] The elements of the scenario were perfect: originally behind the denunciation was Nadia Remadna, a formerly left-wing woman of Maghrebi descent; to this were added female journalists, racialized men, a poor neighborhood, a culturalist explanation (tradition, culture, religion). Even though, after investigation, journalists from the *Bondy Blog*[116] revealed the falseness of this scenario, it took a year before an official at France Télévision admitted to "a bug."[117] Yet, the image had already entered the public debate: contrary to French mores, a tradition, a culture, and a religion were creating a gendered space hostile to women.

The colonial difference between the territory of modernity (the white town) and that of the racialized (*la cité*) played out again. The image of a gendered segregation of public space produced exclusively by men from suburban housing projects invisibilized the other forms of social and racial segregation:

> Lowering their eyes, avoiding catching men's eye, remaining inconspicuous, women are gradually losing their place in the public space. And, by banalizing and accepting this form of violence, we are allowing even more serious forms of violence to be committed. Let's stop closing our eyes. It is by creating a terrain conducive to sexual equality that we shall be able to start eradicating marital, sexual, moral, physical, and many other forms of violence and to thus help victims speak out.[118]

Detain and punish

Appealing to the criminal justice system, and thus encouraging detention, is to perpetuate "the idea that prisons are necessary to democracy and that they are a major part of the solution to social problems."[119] But who is sent to prison? For it "is no secret that prison is used by the State to control non-white and poor populations in particular, making the imprisoned and their families more immiserated, damaging prisoners' physical and mental health, subjecting them to the whims and violence of prison guards and the administration."[120] While women are far less frequently locked up in what are officially designated as prisons (in France, they represent about 4 percent in the places of incarceration run by the prison administration), they are "first and foremost subjected to other forms of social control (overmedicalization, psychiatrization, being taken into care through institutions' 'social' mission, for example in housing shelters, such as the Palais de la femme in Paris). Non-white, precarious, undocumented women, and notably transgender women, are once again over-represented."[121] In the prisons of Île-de-France:

> trans women are often foreigners, locked up for motives concerning the repression and direct or indirect criminalization of the undocumented, of sex work or drug trafficking. For example, the laws attacking female sex workers' working conditions (the 2016 law criminalizing clients; various decrees on parking, whose application targets sex workers; anti-soliciting measures; the future anti-cyberhate law, etc.) makes them more precarious and facilitates targeting them through diverse offenses (mutual aid among sex workers notably can lead to a condemnation for procuring; self-defense can lead to a condemnation for violence, contempt, and obstruction, etc.).[122]

In prison, "young Roma women are treated like males, or even more harshly than them ... Women who completely transgress gender law will also go to prison, such as the 'bad mothers', who have harmed their children."[123] On January 1, 2019, nearly 30 percent of female inmates were foreigners, illiterate, or unschooled beyond primary level, often older than their male counterparts, and proportionally more numerous in pre-trial detention (39 percent versus 28 percent of men).[124] Among these detainees, "many [were] 'mules,' that is, women from French Guiana or elsewhere in South America, who, living in extreme immiseration, have been forced to transport drugs, most frequently in exchange for financial reward."[125] The invisible immured, these women are easily forgotten for, "as women, they are meant to be the upholders of moral order," sociologist Corinne Rostaing observes, continuing:

"Women inmates thus suffer a dual stigmatization: not only have they broken the law, but they have also transgressed the norms relating to their sex. The feeling of shame is greater for women, and their families more often than not turn their backs on them."[126] Anti-foreigner policies, police harassment of the undocumented, and more generally of non-white people, also target trans women via "impossible legal access to a job and housing, and via deportation."[127]

Anti-racist decolonial feminism cannot defend prison, which "masks those in power's bending of the rules, which is no less massive and permanent, but which thereby benefits from impunity or at least a selective tolerance."[128] Prison does not affect just the detainees, but also families and communities, the "real ideological objective of the penal system" being "families rather than individuals."[129] For detainees, vaginal or rectal searches, dehumanization, isolation, boredom, the feeling of being locked away forever, of losing all contact with social life, result in high suicide and self-harming rates, constant recourse to debilitating psychotropic drugs, and difficult re-entry into intimate and social life. For their families, transportation difficulties, prisons' distance and remoteness, the dirty, noisy visiting rooms making all intimacy impossible, all add to the stress and the pain. "A devourer of men and women," prison cannot be reformed.[130] Historically tied to the "first apparatus of education and mass normalization,"[131] the prison model corresponds today to a greater entanglement between neoconservatism and neoliberalism. Prison abolition advocate Angela Davis explains why these reforms never go far enough:

those of us who identify as prison abolitionists, as opposed to prison reformers, make the point that oftentimes reforms create situations where mass incarceration becomes even more entrenched; and so, therefore, we have to think about what in the long run will produce decarceration, fewer people behind bars, and hopefully, eventually, in the future, the possibility of imagining a landscape without prisons, where other means are used to address issues of harm, where social problems, such as illiteracy and poverty, do not lead vast numbers of people along a trajectory that leads to prison.[132]

As one of its architects described, "humanized" prison is above all meant to bring "inmates to accept their condition without revolt."[133] Criticizing prison cannot be a policy; that would be "to exhaust oneself in a struggle that, in a sense, is no longer ours," says Gwenola Ricordeau:[134]

When a wrong is committed, how are we going to collectively place the people who have committed this wrong before their responsibilities and how are we going to repair this wrong for those who suffered it? How are we going to provide solutions so that people do not have to call the police in a situation where they are, or feel, in danger? Envisaging finding solutions to not call the police or to not have to go to file a complaint seems to me far more worthwhile than criticizing prison or partaking in processes to obtain a form of recognition from the State.[135]

By allowing the State the monopoly of conflict resolution, carceral feminism saves women by "judicializing men."[136] "Relying on State violence to curb domestic violence only ends up harming the most marginalized women," writes Victoria Law.[137] We must stop turning to a system—one that claims to save us—that is organized to exclude, lock up, kill. The balance needed between refusing all participation, and engagement in the anti-racist social struggle must be negotiated and found every time, for there is no predetermined path.

84

Conclusion: For a Decolonial Feminist Politics

A world governed by greed and the abuse of power

The systemic and structural violence of racial capitalism and patriarchy was yet again highlighted by the lockdown policies put in place in response to the Covid-19 pandemic.[1] Femicide, assassinations of Indigenous activists,[2] violence against the elderly and children, police violence, and racist violence did not regress anywhere. While the outcome of these policies has not been identical from one country to the next,[3] it is clear that social and racial inequalities and injustices have been exacerbated, which has helped to reveal the immense immiseration caused by the globalization of capitalism and its racial structure. This politics once again underscored the extent to which governments differentiated between those who, having always historically been the object of protection, continued to enjoy this privilege, and the extent to which those who have also historically been constructed as expendable, as surplus, could not only be exposed to the virus and death, but also saw their behavior criminalized. It rapidly became clear that not only were we undergoing a health crisis, but also a political and historical moment that was in no way the fruit of chance.

The epidemic was a disaster foretold. For decades, scientists had been warning governments of the risks posed by the increase in zoonoses, encouraging jumping between species, the multiplication of conditions that favor infectious diseases, and the reduction of research budgets into these diseases. Neoliberal racial capitalism has led us to the abyss: rising sea levels, melting glaciers, increasingly destructive cyclones, droughts, and floods, polluted air and waters, creating a deadly world while at the same time promising a fulfilled, happy life. Breathing has become a class and race privilege: there are now more premature air pollution-related deaths in the world than any other cause.[4] In the months that preceded the first lockdown order alone (January 28, 2020, Wuhan, China), huge environmental destruction took place: fires in California, Siberia, the Congo basin, Amazonia, Indonesia, Australia, and even in the Arctic. Leaders remained unmoved by the smoke and ash that darkened the skies and deposited a layer of grey ash on the earth, landscape, ruins, and even the summits of far-off mountains; by the animals that perished in their millions; by the human beings who were condemned to losing all their goods, to breathing contaminated air, or to being burned alive. These disasters recalled the Union Carbide pesticide plant explosion in Bhopal in 1984, the abandoning of New Orleans' African American community in the wake of the destruction wreaked by Hurricane Katrina in 2005, the women crushed to death at Rana Plaza, Dhaka, Bangladesh in 2013, the lands and racialized communities devastated by chlordecone in the Antilles, the gold-mining industry in French Guiana, or the nickel-extraction industry in Kanaky. The causes and consequences of these catastrophes have been covered up by State lies, the impunity of industrialists, and the absence of reparations. Year after year, dehumanization has become increasingly commonplace.

Government measures have restricted industrial and agrofood activity, causing poverty and hunger, without offering the slightest glimpse of a world not "governed and animated by greed and power," not "deserted by respect and honor," and love.[5] Accordingly, it is without surprise that we learned that the Covid-19 death rate was higher among poor and racialized communities, Black people, Indigenous people, migrants, refugees, prisoners, the homeless, for they could not easily access healthcare, had no medical insurance, and suffered from high comorbidity rates—diabetes, high blood pressure, excess weight—proving that equal access to good health is a mirage. It would have sufficed to revise the history of colonialism and epidemics, of science and racialization, to realize that the socio-economic manipulates the biological. For some of us, the Chikungunya epidemic in Réunion (2005–06) had already illustrated the links between deforestation, capitalism, the multiplication of zoonoses, tourism, austerity programs' undermining of public health services in the Global South, medical research focused on diseases of the North, the incompetence and contempt of the French government, the correlation between the virus' death rate and comorbidity rates relating to poverty, racism, and coloniality. It was with no surprise that we saw the police being given the widest prerogatives to repress racialized communities, and it was with no surprise that we saw the spread of poverty and hunger. The clauses of the extraction and predation-based racial contract[6] and the sexual contract were visible to those who wanted to see them. Lockdown was also preceded by a global protest movement—in Algeria, France, Mexico, Chile, Lebanon, the United States, India, and elsewhere—against police violence, extractivism, climate change, hyper-consumerism, the racial Capitalocene, racism, femicide, and attacks on Indigenous people. These movements courageously confronted the police and invented new forms of protest.

There was no respite from the violence, not a day without news illustrating the destruction, exploitation, and devastation that global racial capitalism causes—the apartheid regime in occupied Palestine, the dismembered, mutilated, burned-alive bodies of women, the daily rapes and assassinations, Black men thrown in prison, and the pollution caused by the chemical and digital industries.

Burn it down!

Les enfants, mettez le feu, mettez le feu!
Mettez le feu pour mettre de l'ordre
Mettez le feu, Mettez le désordre
Mettez le désordre pour mettre de l'ordre.[7]

On March 24, 2018, in Martinique, a land ravaged by the State crime of polluting the earth, rivers, and sea with the pesticide chlordecone, local feminists denounced a form of violence fusing health, colonialism, racism, sexism, environmental crimes, male-female relationships, intergenerational solidarity, and resistance. "Burn it down, bring disorder to bring order," the feminist group #Pebouchfini sang, marching under the banner: "Yesterday enslaved; still exploited. Poisoned today; the women say: Enough!" Adopting the call-and-response rhythm of popular song, they cried: "A healthy earth / (response) That's what we want! / Healthy men, in all respects / That's what we want! / Healthy women / That's what we want! / To be free / That's what we want! / Healthy children / That's what we want!"[8]

Two years later, on March 8, 2020, as the Covid-19 pandemic was spreading around the world, feminists on the main square of Mexico City sang the words of *Song without Fear*, which calls out the justice system, the State, the patriarchy, and the police's complicity in femicide:

Let the State, the skies, the streets tremble
Let the judges, the magistrature tremble
Today women have lost their calm

...

And let the earth tremble at its core
Before our roars of love.[9]

It was in this context—that of the constructive anger and rage of social movements around the world, of the faster than anticipated acceleration of the destruction of the environment, of France's unlocking of the first stage of the health emergency announced by the government on March 17, 2020, of the rise in social and racial inequalities and injustices, of increased opportunities for the neoliberal economy and the security-based and militarized State—that I was writing my conclusion to this book. While nourished by all that was written at the time about the lies, delays, governments' class, and racial contempt, my argument here has focused on the systemic violence that ruins our existences and destroys the conditions necessary for the maintaining of human life. This violence is economic and social, psychological and cultural. Government lockdown and post-lockdown programs have ushered in the considerable development of digital capitalism and restrictions on mobility, exchanges, and meeting one another. A vast social engineering program was put in place from the very start of lockdown, and no one can guarantee that it will not be permanent. It deeply affects human interactions and intergenerational solidarity, as witnessed in France with old people's condemnation to a lonely death with no affectionate hand to comfort them. This program encourages denunciations, suspicion, and stress. Many are those who said they went to work with their "stomachs knotted," and who have had to face great aggressivity sparked by the worry and fear. Governments dream of docile, domesticated, and privatized lives. Reading the perspectives outlined by bankers, financiers, businesspeople, and financial advisors, all the virtuous declarations about a change of paradigm appear totally fictional. We have been warned: massive restructuring is on the horizon, heightened surveillance and control, and the development of what Naomi Klein calls the "Screen New Deal," that is, the growth of surveillance and control industries, of online education and healthcare, the privatization of the healthcare system, etc.[10]

During lockdown, what Black feminists, feminists from the Global South, materialist feminists, or racialized trade unionists had explained for decades—that racialized women are the bedrock upon which societies build their comfort—was at last recognized by academics, journalists, politicians, and thus mediatized. In Brazil, the United States, Singapore, or in France, bourgeoise women were forced to recognize that their well-being and their feminism—when they claimed to be feminist—depended on these women's work. Their world appeared for what it is: of a filthiness allegedly compensated for by this planetary bourgeoisie's hygienist concerns, unlike the poor and racialized communities, said to neglect their environment and homes out of laziness. Yet the concepts of cleanliness and dirt are not neutral; people do not have equal access to water, soap, to an ecologically healthy habitat. Water is inaccessible to migrants, to the homeless, to prisoners; in Guadeloupe, the Prefect even had to organize a water distribution by tanker![11]

Hygiene has a racial and class history. In her description of the state of the hotel rooms that racialized women workers must clean, Rachel Kélé, one of the women strikers at the Ibis Accor Batignolles Hotel in Paris,[12] underlined the relation between racialized women, exploitation, dirtiness, and cleanliness: the cleaning women find rooms in which clients have left behind vomit, dirty toilets, traces of blood or excrement, crumbs from meals, clothes thrown on the floor; the cleaners sometimes need two to three binbags to empty a room. Adding these expressions of contempt to those of the Accor Group and the subcontractor who employs them, to the 30 to 50 rooms to clean a day, at a rate of one room every 17 minutes for a salary of €800 to 900 (approx. $1,000) a month, to a job that "injures" and "exhausts," to the link between racialization and invisibilization, to their suffering at not being able to give their children the education they want and the presents they deserve, Rachel Kélé demonstrates the importance of combining feelings, emotions, and facts to as precisely as possible describe the structural violence inflicted on them.[13] Their invisibilization, the lack of respect for their work, their low wages, the exploitation and racism that mark the "frontline" jobs that racialized women do, are all founded on the long history of the process of social reproduction and racialized society's comfort.

These facts are a concentration of the social and racial architecture of bourgeois homes or the spaces of capital, or the State: a racialized person is owed no respect; people can display their filth with no shame, exhibit elements of their private life, and even take pleasure in doing so as they get a kick out of contributing to racialized people's humiliation, to the refusal to allow them their dignity. During colonial slavery, plantation owners—both women and men—would unhesitatingly speak about private matters or reveal themselves in the most intimate of situations in front of the enslaved, as did—and still do—the bourgeois in front of their servants, or as people still do today in front of salespeople, security guards, cleaning women, sex workers. Bourgeois civility and cleanliness are masks that rely on devolving cleaning and care to the racialized, on the exhaustion of their bodies and their strength, and thus inevitably on the fabrication of bodies in poorer health.

Healthy bodies, which are the measure of public health policies, are historically marked by racism and class. Racialized bodies are socio-historic bodies. Speaking of "invisible" bodies and lives does not imply asking for recognition from the powerful, but rather rejecting the historically racialized and sexualized regime of visibility. Decolonial and anti-racist feminist struggles against violence imply understanding that the latter is not the result of male domination alone, but of a system that turns violence into a way of life and existence, which institutes it as the only mode of relation. By declaring war on the State, the police, judges, by making the good health of the earth and those that inhabit it the condition of a peaceful life, by highlighting the necessity of their work cleaning the world, these feminists and women-in-struggle stress the multidisciplinary, transversal, transborder, and internationalist facet of feminist liberation struggles.

Wounded lives

Every day, dominant culture directly or subliminally proposes the image of what it is "to be a woman" and "to be a man," and this man, this woman, are high-classed, white (or whitened), and healthy. To analyze violence is to take into account the fact that male domination exerts itself on women *and* on men. Colonial slavery was the matrix of the binarism that founds domination between genders and within genders.[14] Inseparable from Western modernity, from the development of capitalism, from Western countries' militarization of the seas and oceans, colonial slavery regulated the modern international laws that govern the ownership of land, plants, animals, and bodies. The white man became a pioneer, a discoverer of lands, an explorer of territories that were "virgin" to him alone. The white woman became fragile and delicate, the opposite of the white man, but also of the Black woman. Slavery transformed Black women's and men's bodies into sexual objects, into bodies to be trafficked and massacred, raped, humiliated, and exploited until death. They were the terrain of cultural and political maneuvers, laboratory objects to be dissected and disfigured. Yet although colonial slavery fixed gender, it "troubled" it too. It racialized gender and was "blind" to it (as capitalism can be). Black women were constructed as hard-working, as incapable of maternal feelings, love, and affection *and* as capable of nourishing and taking care of white people. They were white children's nannies, a job in which white women expected them to be gentle and loving. An enslaved Black woman was a body-object of the female sex and a genderless and unsexed body to exploit like that of an enslaved man. Black women were the victims of repeated rape as "women" and as "slaves"; they were tortured in the same way as Black men.[15] They were assigned the hardest labor in the fields *and* worked in the kitchens and serving. Black men were constructed as sexualized brutes, as beings incapable of understanding techniques *and* as those to whom the slaveholders confided the working of their mills, or the highly-qualified position of coachman or slave driver. The invention of white virility was based on the criminalization of racialized masculine bodies, misogyny, Negrophobia, and Orientalism. Racialized men's ability to love and articulate complex discourses is still questioned. A linguist, whose academic legitimacy is uncontested, can freely claim: "The common trend among young people from the neighborhoods is the use of short sentences ... Complex sentences, with main and subordinate clauses, are never used, which can give the appearance of a unique rhythm. Lexical paucity and poor mastery of syntax also encourage using the same forms of fragments of rigid discourse."[16] The very fact that the circumstances of murders of racialized young people are never fully elucidated, that investigations come to nothing, that requests for an expertise are refused, that the murderers remain unpunished, all add to the violence. In white supremacy's view, the gender of non-white people is both fixed and fluid, as gender binarism is an attribute of whiteness. Racialized women are not completely "women" and racialized men are not completely "men," according to the norms inherited from slavery and colonialism.[17] That is what is spelled out by the concept of "misogynoir," that is, the specific misogyny targeting

Black women, who are denigrated in sexist, racist, and/or colorist attacks.[18] Added to these reflections are the analyses of feminists of the Global South attacking male chauvinism and sexism, based on their critique of the "prioritization of struggles." To take into account this racialized organization of gender and bodies, and the existence of masculinities, femininities, and non-binary genders, is to also become aware of the testimonies of racialized men concerning their refusal of violence as proof of their "masculinity"; it is to adopt a multi-directional method of analysis. By maintaining the binary male/female division, punitive carceral feminism does not attack the structural racism underlying this binarity. As long as struggles against gender-based and sexual violence are based on the categories of "women" and "men" forged and nourished by racism and sexism, and as they are upheld by the State, they do not contribute to liberation struggles.

"Never let a good crisis go to waste"

Neoliberalism has never been just an economic program; it aims for a cultural transformation of the self, in which the school system and socialization play a major role.[19] It is a "constructivist" program that seeks to subjugate people and their environment.[20] Neoliberals do not aspire to the destruction of the State, but rather to its subjugation, its transformation into an active, central tool of the fabrication of subjectivities, social relations, and collective representations. They readily, and simultaneously, adopt contradictory positions,[21] as exemplified by the Macronist "at the same time" rhetoric, such as, for example, making speeches in defense of women's rights while at the same time passing laws that make them—and more specifically racialized women—more vulnerable to poverty and violence. Their lies, their incompetence, their absurd or empty declarations, must not blind us to their objectives; we must also ask ourselves what post-pandemic society capitalism is preparing for us, what forms of social interaction the State will authorize, and how their measures will reinforce mistrust, suspicion, denunciation in the aim of calming social anger, and how the prevention of the health crisis facilitates the setting up of a "technopolice" and a world police State.[22] It heralds a vast social engineering project in which regulation, laws, and ideology aim to discipline individual and social behaviors.

While neither neoliberals nor the governments that serve them were expecting the Covid-19 pandemic, it was not long before they saw an opportunity in the lockdowns—that of making profit, of accelerating the development of digital capitalism, and, accordingly, of reducing labor costs. Their profits were already visible as early as January 2020: the fortune of Eric Yuan, CEO of Zoom, the application that facilitated online meetings and videoconferences, exploded,[23] as did that of Amazon founder Jeff Bezos.[24]

With every "crisis," the coercive powers of the State are extended, the economy restructured, the social-racial space reordered. Having led us to the brink, the State and neoliberals surmount the crisis by having us accept human losses among the poorest and racialized classes and by intensifying technological advances. "Militarized accumulation" has become a global fact,[25] and the global economy is "ever more dependent on the development and deployment of systems of warfare, social control and repression, apart from political considerations, simply as a means of making profit and continuing to accumulate capital in the face of stagnation."[26] In France, the idea of a continuum between the forms of security guaranteed by the State and those developed by the private sector is finding increasing support among parliamentarians and government. Facial recognition techniques even when the face is covered,[27] drones, cameras, geolocalization, database filing, and phone tapping are fueling an already highly lucrative market. At the end of 2018, "the world security market displayed an insolent growth rate of 7%, well above the 2% world growth rate, attaining a turnover of 629 billion euros."[28] In the name of security for all, protection is being militarized, behavior penalized, and communities criminalized. What guarantee do we have that the protection of women and their freedom of movement will not be based on this militarization of the public, and even private space?

War, which is at the heart of the construction of the modern world, which constitutes the very basis of colonial and imperialist politics, is the central weapon of structural, systemic violence, of racial and neoliberal capitalism, and its patriarchy. The "we" of government rhetoric is a fictitious we.[29] The language of war saturates our existence and the wars "on drugs and terrorism; the undeclared wars on immigrants, refugees, gangs, and poor, dark-skinned and working-class youth more generally; the construction of border walls, immigrant jails, prison-industrial complexes, systems of mass surveillance, and the spread of private security guard and mercenary companies have all become major sources of profit-making."[30]

A decolonial feminism cannot ignore these facts. It cannot forget that France's "war on terrorism" found the references to naturalize and racialize the surveillance and control of Muslims in Orientalism, demonizing the hijab, turning mosques and Muslim schools into dangerous places which are "by nature" hostile to freedom and equality. It had us accept bag checks and body searches, the militarized control of spaces, abusive identity checks, house arrests and abusive detention of Muslims. It came as no surprise that the pandemic and its lockdown policies were racialized in France, as they were elsewhere. Anti-Asian, anti-African, anti-Muslim racism have not only served as outlets, but have served as justification for geopolitical and national decisions. By April 20, 2020, five people had already died in France and more than ten were seriously injured following police arrests in poor racialized neighborhoods,[31] and in these areas, twice as many identity checks were carried out than the national average, and three times as many fines were handed out.[32] On April 20, seven complaints were filed for police violence: "In addition to racist insults, unwanted touching, and humiliations, several victims of this police violence recounted that they thought they were dying, that they could no longer breathe, that they were scared for their lives."[33] On the night of April 25–26, a video showed French police sneering and joking after a young man they were chasing jumped in the river Seine on the Île-Saint-Denis: "In the film, which lasts a little less than three minutes, we see one of the policemen saying: 'He doesn't know how to swim, *bicots* can't swim.' This is met with laughter, then another policeman responds: "They sink. You should have put a ball and chain around his foot.'"[34] It is likely that these policemen had no knowledge of the October 17, 1961 march when they made their jokes, but somewhere, the echo of the French police's murderous actions in 1961 are etched into police memory.[35]

Before the deluge of pronouncements about the world after, how to think about the past, present, and future without subjecting oneself to the temporality of Western modernity? How to refuse the injunction of the future when it demands an erasure of the present without reparations? "Collectively or individually, we are deprived of projects, incapable of imagining a future beyond the next few days. Yet, to live as a fully human person is to project oneself."[36] Is it a privilege to imagine? The *Pas sans Nous* (Not Without Us) collective thinks so: "Whether the sincerest like it or not, imagining the 'world after,' remains a luxury in poor neighborhoods," for "to dream of the after, the present already needs to be decent ... Yet daily life remains one of indecency, of social and ecological injustice, of stigmatization. Coronavirus or not, the future here is never really tangible and the horizon precisely often an unsurmountable hurdle."[37] Imagining a *post*-(slavery, racist, capitalist, imperialist, patriarchal) future is nonetheless a powerful weapon in the hands of the oppressed. Daring to make the leap in time, daring to imagine a world in which humanity is not divided into lives that matter and lives that do not, has always been a part of the political pedagogy of the oppressed. Revolutionary winds counter the "there is no alternative," "it's always been this way," "you can't change human nature," "there have always been the strong and the weak," "it's in women's nature." To dare to imagine is to reject Western time's opposition of past, present, and future, which is not that of communities or non-Western peoples, nor of struggles. These multiple temporalities are irreducible: they have that virtue of repairing a past woven out of massacres, destruction, and crimes; of repairing a present in which massacres, destruction, and crimes are the organizing elements of government; of repairing a future in which the effects of past and present violence are already foreseeable. These alternative temporalities are those of an anti-racist, decolonial feminism. Decolonial timeframes are based on realities: a slaving, racist, and colonialist past; a present of exploitation, racism, and oppression; a future that announces forms of exploitation and oppression combining the techniques of surveillance, control, and racism; and domination of the past and present, and those imagined in the future. The timeframe of decolonial struggles are also the long-term temporality of the struggles, revolts, insurrections, and revolutions of the past and those of present, and of the utopias of liberation. They question the temporal binarity of power, which mirrors that of war. While it is necessary to organize to meet material urgencies— hunger, unemployment, paying the rent, sending children to school, fighting against the bankruptcy of family business in poor neighborhoods—to which are added the need to reduce stress, worries, health problems, work problems, and personal problems, we cannot ignore that what is in preparation—and which will first of all affect the working classes and racialized communities—demands that we imagine a future.

An anti-racist, cross-border decolonial feminist politics of protection

In response to the macabre daily litany of femicides, to the stories of bodies dismembered, stabbed, suffocated, tortured, mutilated, burned alive, thrown in dumps, feminist self-defense organizations have formed. Confronted with the indifference and contempt of governments and the powerful, feminist collectives are resorting to direct action. Shouting one's anger is no longer enough, declared Carolina Barrales of the *Circulo Violeta* feminist collective based in Tijuana, Mexico: "We won't just sit around quietly waiting for another woman to be murdered or for another girl to be raped … we believe in smashing whatever needs to be smashed, shouting whatever you need to shout, doing whatever you need to do."[38] But the powerful remain unpunished; when they are finally charged, the trial takes place in the courthouse, a patriarchal, sexist, and racist institution in which magistrates and lawyers play their role and in which women's words are inscribed in a scenario over which they have little control. The script is truncated and there are many women who describe feeling that justice has not been done. In response to these offenses, the patriarchs reorganize and repress, undermine rights or enact laws that make brutality and force a right.[39] The myth of freedom of expression of speaking out,[40] the distinction made between "peaceful" feminist demonstrations—in other words, respecting the norms dictated by the holders of power—and demonstrations that do not respect these norms and can thus be violently repressed once again show that what protesting women say and want must remain within the boundaries of the bourgeois respectability of women's rights in order to be tolerated—a distinction made clear in 2020 France. On March 7, 2020, in Paris, during a "non-mixed night march"—that is, reserved to women, racialized and trans people—organized by militant collectives distinct from those who called to rally on Sunday, March 8, the demonstrators sang: "We are strong, we are proud, and feminist and radical and enraged." When they reached the Place de la République, they were kettled and tear-gassed by the police, dragged by their hair, pinned to the ground, hit, insulted, dragged down the subway steps by heavily armed police, and detained in police custody. To justify this, the Paris Prefect denounced a "hostile mood towards the police." After having tweeted "All women must be allowed to demonstrate peacefully for the respect of their rights!", Marlène Schiappa, the Secretary of State for Equality between Men and Women added in justification of the police intervention: "We are talking about a night march, organized by antifascist, anticapitalist, feminist groups who decided to hold a nighttime demonstration ... The report requested by the Minister of the Interior indicates that the demonstration route appears not to have been respected and that this led to the events witnessed here."[41] Contrastingly, the March 8 demonstration in Paris was presented as peaceful and thus respectable. However true that characterization might or might not have been, what is certain is that the repression of the March 7 feminist rally was justified by the police and the government, whereas the March 8 rally, fitting the "women's rights" frame, and thereby erasing the historical revolutionary nature of an "international women's day" designed to mark women's struggle, was deemed acceptable. The distinction between anti-fascist and anti-capitalist feminism and women's rights feminism was highlighted here, the latter being perceived as appropriate as it does not frontally attack capitalism, but rather *a* patriarchy—macho, retrograde, and anti-modern. Respectability demands a lot of cosmetics, and a strong capacity to endure humiliation. We can safely bet that all the indignant declarations about the inequalities affecting women will not translate into an attack on racial capitalism. Let it not be forgotten that the application of legislation protecting women during the Welfare State period in Europe did not transform the gendered and racialized division of labor.[42] Fighting violence of course means demanding that the State fund emergency shelters, but that cannot be the end objective of an anti-racist, decolonial feminism. I have expressed my lack of confidence in the State and the judicial machine's ability to provide protection several times in this book. Let us heed the words of Angela Davis:

> How then can one expect the state to solve the problem of violence against women, when it constantly recapitulates its own history of colonialism, racism, and war? How can we ask the state to intervene when, in fact, its armed forces have always practiced rape and battery against "enemy" women? In fact, sexual and intimate violence against women has been a central military tactic of war and domination. Yet the approach of the neoliberal state is to incorporate women into these agencies of violence—to integrate the armed forces and the police.[43]

That femicide and systemic violence now exist at the heart of current demonstrations and reflections shows that the idea of the entanglement of different forms of racism, sexism, transphobia, homophobia, class violence, of the systematic destruction of the environment necessary for human life, is increasingly widely accepted. What to do then? Demand from the State what it owes us while nonetheless remaining autonomous, state our conditions when we enter into dialogue with institutions, set things alight, create disorder, collectively educate ourselves (Education! Education! Education!), show solidarity with all liberation struggles, nurture revolutionary friendship and love.[44]

The unrelenting violence has become unbearable.[45] What Achille Mbembe calls "brutalism" has become the iron law governing the human condition.[46] This law demands that we be constantly on the lookout, anxious, that we barricade ourselves in "at home," haunted by the fear of invasion, terrorized by the unexpected, accepting the calm we are offered at the price of lives whose dignity is refused. One of the consequences of war is to drive women and men onto the roads of exile in a permanent race to find a place to lay down their heads, to close their eyes in confidence, to enjoy a moment of respite. Evoking the right to a peaceful life in a violent world may seem naïve and unrealistic, as war has been naturalized and peace reduced to an interlude between two violent moments, to a negotiation between armies and States, to a "ceasefire," and as the media have normalized the bombings, the criminalization of childhood,[47] the deaths with no graves, the decimated cities, the refugees persecuted and treated like surplus populations. The right to a peaceful life does not mean a life without joy and fervor, but the capacity to exercise one's imagination, to allow oneself to daydream, to partake in aimless activities, or activities that require time and patience. It is not by chance that one method of torture is to prevent people from resting. This *right to rest* is combatted by States that declare war on the simplest of gestures that constitute a peaceable relationship between human beings: giving someone a glass of water or food, assisting the wounded, indicating a safe path, saving people from drowning. More than shelter, it is this right to rest, to a peaceful life, that needs to be developed to counter violence. We need to dare to dream of a peaceful life. Peaceful, here, does not mean pacification or appeasing, but a politics and a practice of solidarity, love, and self-defense. It is a form of life that does not preclude feeling anger at injustices and racism, but which develops our self- and revolutionary love. A heightened awareness of State violence, of the weight of colonialism and racism on bodies and minds, and of the importance of *all* forms of struggle, however "small" they are, animates a decolonial feminism. It never minimizes the courage it takes to refuse the State's offers of respectability—which, for its part, proposes only one way out of the coloniality of being and racist contempt: to wear the white mask. This learning of the long-term temporality of struggle, its form of respiration, its patience, and its determination, its violence and its generosity, is what authentically guides our decolonial feminism.

State violence / autonomous defense

The construction of a peaceful world absolutely does not imply passivity. Mexican feminists' response to State violence on March 8, 2020[48]—throwing Molotov cocktails at the presidential residence, confronting the police—the March 7, 2020 feminist march in Paris to cries of "The party's over, the feminists are out!", "Stand up, rise up!",[49] the legitimate anger of France's working-class racialized neighborhoods in response to police violence in April 2020, the organization, under the *Nunca más sin nosotras* (Never Again Without Us Women) banner, of demonstrations in Chile from November 2019 to March 2020 with members of *Primera Linea* protecting demonstrators from police charges, the tactics of the huge demonstrations in Algeria, Lebanon, France: all these demonstrate a deep understanding that institutionalized nonviolence and the politics of respectability do not protect. It is not that institutional brutality has suddenly appeared over the last few months, but that it is increasingly clear that the State does not seek to protect its citizens. Without *Primera Linea*, the violence of the Chilean State would have been more murderous, declared activist Ale Bórquez Bravo: "Without them, we wouldn't have achieved any gains in the past, and we wouldn't have been able to mobilize such large numbers of people."[50] To combat violence against women is to combat the consubstantial violence of the State and of capitalism, which maintain the impunity of gender and racial violence. If it were not already clear enough, the Covid-19 lockdown revealed the fact that home is not a refuge; all countries saw an increase in the number of calls to helplines reporting violence (a 30 percent increase in France, while in the UK, 16 women were killed by a male partner or relative between late March and mid-April 2020). But while this violence may take place in any home, bourgeois or poor, shoddily built, cramped, working-class housing that is poorly maintained by the authorities exacerbates it.

In this age of systemic and globalized violence, State civilizational feminism plays the role of a pacifying ideology that aims to break the momentum of women's anger. Just as we have come to understand the importance of the "wages of whiteness,"[51] we now understand the importance of the wages of white, bourgeois, civilizational, State feminism, which guarantee both privileges and the illusion of mattering, of having accessed a little spot among the powerful, while the latter only grant this on the condition of not challenging their existence. This wage contributes to the structuring of racial and economic domination. This feminism, which sees the State as synonymous with security and protection, encourages calls for ever more criminal laws and thus, inevitably, more police and prisons, for this patriarchal and capitalist State's conception of justice is based on punishment. Their feminism manages to mask its participation in the mechanisms of domination very well but "if we refuse to consider specifically female modes of assimilating [and taking] power, we will not be able to understand how conservative forces manage to turn identitarian demands to their advantage."[52] Civilizational feminists play the effective role of neocolonial administrators. Immunized against calls to their consciences, the powerful occasionally concede a little, but these concessions are never achieved by respectability politics. Either they are scared, or such progress costs them nothing, or they ensure that no institution will guarantee that the laws voted for are applied, or that the sexist and racist ideology of capitalism will be stronger than the laws voted for.[53] Only struggle forces those in power to make concessions.

We can, then, revisit the epic narrative of the European feminist movements' demonstrations in the 1960s and 1970s. Without denying the determination of the women who participated, the contribution of radical feminist groups would not be overlooked, nor that—fundamental—of racialized women in the North and those of the Global South, who, with their struggles for total liberation, challenged the powerful and white supremacy. These feminists, who always made clear the difference between the violence of oppression and of liberation, and who always distinguished between the violence of white supremacist patriarchy and that of their communities' male chauvinism, knew that fighting a State that deploys pesticides that poison the earth, animals, plants, and humans, a State that has militarized the public space, entrusted private militias with maintaining its order, is also to combat violence against women. To combat these forms of violence is to fight against the army and its politics of rape, it is to fight against shops, cultural institutions, universities, and schools that continue to circulate racist and sexist images and representations. It is to forge alliances with men, with non-binary people, with queer people, with trans people who fight against virilism and racism. It is to forge alliances with feminists who fully embark on a process of decolonizing and deracializing their theories and practices. In France, it is young men from poor neighborhoods, backed by their families, their communities, and by associations often run by racialized women (*Urgence notre police assassine*, *Le comité la Vérité pour Adama*), who, by courageously opposing the militarized police, scare the State and reveal that its violence and brutality are structural. It is Black, racialized women who go on strike, create collectives, demonstrate, fight racism and capitalism one step at a time, who challenge universalist and State feminism. The question is not about being pro-violence or pro-non-violence, but about refusing the bourgeois condemnation of the violence of the oppressed and favoring a multiplicity of tactics and thus the flexibility and autonomy of struggle.[54] If there are lessons to be learned from the systemic violence that preceded the politics of lockdown decreed in early 2020, and from the global deterioration of racial, gender, sex, age, and class inequalities and injustices, it is that we are living in an era in which it is impossible to escape the unleashing of uncontrollable violence produced by greed, cupidity, and power unless we organize alongside those who have nothing to lose.

Notes

Introduction

1. Diane Sprimont, "'*Un violador en tu camino*' : voici les paroles en français du chant féministe chilien devenu hymne mondial," *France Inter*, December 10, 2019, www.franceinter.fr/societe/un-violador-en-tu-camino-voici-les-paroles-en-francais-du-chant-feministe-chilien-devenu-hymne-mondial; Justine Fontaine, "Au Chili, le slam qui blâme les violeurs," *Libération*, December 20, 2019, www.liberation.fr/planete/2019/12/20/au-chili-le-slam-qui-blame-les-violeurs_1770502, accessed January 9, 2020.

2. Various English versions of the lyrics exist, for example: www.lifegate.com/the-rapist-is-you-un-violador-en-tu-camino, or https://womensmarch.com/2020-dance, accessed May 7, 2021.

3. Darinka Rodriguez, "Ellas son las chilenas que crearon 'Un violador en tu camino'," *Verne*, November 28, 2019, https://verne.elpais.com/verne/2019/11/28/mexico/1574902455_578060.html, accessed January 25, 2020; D. Sprimont, "'*Un violador en tu camino*.'"

4. Elsa Dorlin, *Se défendre* (Paris: La Découverte, 2019), e-book, emplacement 1097.

5. Sayak Valencia, in Ella Bordai, "La violence devient un écosystème et un système de production de sens: la mort,"', November 3, 2009, *Réseau d'études décoloniales*, http://reseaudecolonial.org/2019/11/03/sayak-valencia-le-regime-necroscopique-de-la-culture-narco-est-aussi-un-regime-economique-qui-alimente-des-niches-importantes-du-marche-global-%EF%80%AA/

6. Ruth Wilson Gilmore, *Golden Gulag. Prisons, Surplus, Crisis and Opposition in Globalizing California* (Berkeley: University of California Press, 2007), p. 247.

7. A concept developed in Françoise Vergès' *A Decolonial Feminism* (London: Pluto Press, 2021).

8. Elizabeth Bernstein, "The Sexual Politics of the New Abolitionism," *Differences*, 2007, 18(5): 128–51. See also: Elizabeth Bernstein, "Militarized Humanitarianism Meets Carceral Feminism: The Politics of Sex, Rights, and Freedom in Contemporary Antitrafficking Campaigns," *Signs: Journal of Women in Culture and Society*, 2010, 36(1): 45–71.

9. In Donald Trump's words.

1 Neoliberal Violence

1. Centre audiovisuel Simone de Beauvoir, Paris, 1985. https://base.centre-simone-de-beauvoir.com/DIAZ-510-17-0-0.html

2. Or what Maria Lugones called their "intermeshing."

3. Jeanne Bisilliat, "Les logiques d'un refus. Les femmes rurales africaines et les politiques d'ajustement structurel," *Les Cahiers du Genre*, "Les paradoxes de la mondialisation," 1998, 21: 95–109, p. 100.

4. Ibid.

5. *8Mars.info* website.

6. E. Dorlin, *Se défendre*, e-book p. 1097.

7. Ruth Wilson Gilmore, citing Allen Feldman, *Formations of Violence: The Narrative of the Body and Political Terror in Northern Ireland* (Chicago, IL and London: University of Chicago Press, 1991), p. 25.

8. Benoist Rey, *Les Égorgeurs* (Saint-Georges-d'Oléron: Les Éditions libertaires, 2012), p. 15.

9. *Le Monde* and AFP, "Casques bleus accusés d'abus sexuels: l'ONU fait monter la pression sur les pays fournisseurs de troupes," May 18, 2016, www.lemonde.fr/international/article/2016/05/18/quarante-quatre-cas-d-abus-sexuels-commis-par-des-casques-bleus-recenses-depuis-debut-2016_4921116_3210.html

10. A report revealed that the soldiers had tortured Iraqi detainees, "beating detainees with a broom handle and a chair; threatening

male detainees with rape; allowing a military police guard to stitch the wound of a detainee who was injured after being slammed against the wall in his cell; sodomizing a detainee with a chemical light and perhaps a broom stick, and using military working dogs to frighten and intimidate detainees with threats of attack, and in one instance actually biting a detainee." See Seymour Hersch's article, "Torture at Abu Ghraib," *New Yorker*, April 30, 2004, www.newyorker.com/magazine/2004/05/10/torture-at-abu-ghraib

11. Coco Fusco, *Petit Manuel de torture à l'usage des femmes soldats* (Paris: Les Prairies ordinaires, 2008), p. 57.

12. Ibid., p. 63.

13. Ibid., p. 95.

14. Mervyn Christian, Octave Safari, Paul Ramazani, Gilbert Burnham, and Nancy Glass, "Sexual and gender based violence against men in the Democratic Republic of Congo: Effects on survivors, their families and the community," *Journal of Medicine, Conflict and Survival*, 2011, 27(4): 227–46, p. 233, www.tandfonline.com/doi/ref/10.1080/13623699.2011.645144?scroll=top

15. See Daniel Summers, "'Rectal feeding' has nothing to do with nutrition and everything to do with torture," *Daily Beast*, April 14, 2017, www.thedailybeast.com/rectal-feeding-has-nothing-to-do-with-nutrition-everything-to-do-with-torture; Hayes Brown, "CIA used 'rectal feeding' as part of torture program," *BuzzFeed. News*, December 9, 2014, www.buzzfeednews.com/article/hayesbrown/cia-used-rectal-feeding-as-part-of-torture-program; Brian Merchant, "Rectal feeding: The antiquated medical practice the cia used for torture," *MotherBoard*, December 9, 2014, www.vice.com/en_us/article/3dk59v/rectal-feeding-the-obsolete-medical-practice-the-cia-used-as-torture; Alan Yuhas, "Controversial 'rectal feeding' technique used to control detainees' behaviour," *The Guardian*, December 9, 2014, www.theguardian.com/us-news/2014/dec/09/cia-report-rectal-feeding-detainees

16. *Report of the Senate Committee on Intelligence, Committee Study of the Central Intelligence Agency's Detention and Interrogation Program*, December 9, 2014, p. 4, https://www.intelligence.

senate.gov/sites/default/files/publications/CRPT-113srpt288.
pdf.

17. Bordai, "La violence devient un écosystème et un système de production de sens."

18. "Les complicités européennes dans le programme des prisons secrètes de la CIA," *Amnesty*, February 3, 2020. www.amnesty.be/infos/blogs/blog-paroles-chercheurs-defenseurs-victimes/article/complicites-europeennes-program-torture-prisons-secretes

19. Ibid.

20. Jérémie Pham-Lê, "Affaire Théo: Une expertise révèle des séquelles à vie pour le jeune homme," *Le Parisien*, August 29, 2019, www.leparisien.fr/faits-divers/affaire-theo-une-expertise-revele-des-sequelles-a-vie-pour-le-jeune-homme-29-08-2019-8141895.php

21. Cited by Verena Hölzl, "Male rape survivors go uncounted in Rohingya camps," *The New Humanitarian*, September 4, 2019, www.thenewhumanitarian.org/news-feature/2019/09/04/Rohingya-men-raped-Myanmar-Bangladesh-refugee-camps-GBV, and her report to the UN: "'It's happening to our men as well': Sexual violence against Rohingya men and boys", November 2018, www.un.org/sexualviolenceinconflict/wp-content/uploads/report/auto-draft/Rohingya-Report-Final-pdf

22. V. Hölzl, "Male rape survivors."

23. M. Christian et al., "Sexual and gender-based violence,", p. 233.

24. Ibid., p. 234.

25. Ibid., p. 235.

26. Sayak Valencia, *Gore Capitalism* (Pasadena, CA: Semiotexte (e), 2018), e-book.

27. Ibid.

28. Ibid.

29. Paul B. Preciado, "La nécropolitique à la française," *Libération*, November 22, 2013, www.liberation.fr/france/2013/11/22/la-necropolitique-a-la-francaise_961371

30. Fanon, *Black Skin, White Masks*, trans. Charles Lam Markmann (New York: Grove Press, 1967), p. 10.

31. Rita Segato, cited by Jules Falquet, in Chapter 14 "L'État néolibéral et les femmes. Le cas du 'bon élève' mexicain," in idem (ed.), *Le sexe de la mondialisation. Genre, classe, race et nouvelle division du travail* (Paris: Presses de Sciences Po, 2010), pp. 229–42, p. 238;; See also, "En Amérique latine, il y avait un féminisme décolonial avant le boom du courant décolonial," interview with Margara Millan by Luis Martinez Andrade, November 4, 2019, http://reseaudecolonial.org/2019/11/04/en-amerique-latine-peut-on-parler-de-lexistence-dun-feminisme-decolonial-anterieur-au-boom-du-courant-decolonial

32. C. Fusco, *Petit Manuel de torture à l'usage des femmes soldats*, p. 34.

33. Valencia, *Gore Capitalism*.

34. Ivan Ketsere, "Dehumanising the Other: The language of black-on-black racism," *Daily Maverick*, September 9, 2019, https://dailymaverick.co.za/article/2019-09-09

35. Bidaseca, Karina (ed.), *Escritos en los cuerpos racializados. Lenguas, memoria y genealogías (pos)coloniales del femininicido*, Collecció Estudis de Violència de gènere (Palma: Edicions Universitat de les Illes Balears, 2015), cited by Rosa Campoalegra Septien, "Féminicide: l'essentiel ne doit être ni invisible ni invincible," October 16, 2018, trans. Fernando Vasquez, http://reseaudecolonial.org/2018/10/16/femicide-lessentiel-ne-doit-etre-ni-invisible-ni-invincible/

36. Roswitha Scholz, *Le Sexe du capitalisme, "masculinité" et "féminité" comme piliers du patriarcat producteur de marchandises* (Albi: Crise & Critique, 2019), trans. Sandrine Aumercie, p. 109.

37. Ibid.; see also Preciado, "La nécropolitique à la française. "

38. Martha Zapata Galindo, "Modernización, poder y cultura: cambios en la relación de los intelectuales mexicanos hacia la política, el gobernio y el Estado", in Nikolaus Böttcher, Isabel Galaor and Bernd Hausberger (eds.), *Los buenos, los malos y los feos: Poder y resistancia en América Latina* (Madrid and Frankfurt am Main: Iberoamericana-Vervuet, 2005), pp. 83–104.

39. Mathieu Magnaudeix, "Dans les McDonald's américains, une grève historique contre les violences sexuelles," *Mediapart*, September 21, 2018, www.mediapart.fr/journal/international/210918/dans-les-mcdonald-s-americains-une-

greve-historique-contre-les-violences-sexuelles?
onglet=full

40. Ibid.

41. Equal Rights Advocates tweet, September 18, 2018. https://
twitter.com/EqualRightsAdv/status/1042149638843715584,
cited in "MeToo #TimesUp: Les salariées de McDonald's
dénoncent les abus sexuels lors d'une grève inédite," *TV5Monde*,
September 20, 2018, https://information.tv5monde.com/
terriennes/metoo-timesup-les-salariees-de-mcdonald-s-
denoncent-les-abus-sexuels-lors-d-une-greve

42. On the rape, see Tatiana Lima, "Du vol des salariées au viol d'une
femme de chambre: grève à l'hôtel Ibis Batignolles," *Révolution
permanente*, July 24, 2019, www.revolutionpermanente.fr/Du-vol-
des-salariees-au-viol-d-une-femme-de-chambre-greve-a-l-hotel-
Ibis-de-Batignolles, and Eric Fassin, Eric Coquerel and Clémentine
Autain, "L'esclavage c'ets fini, même pour les femmes de
chambre," *Libération*, March 9, 2020, www.liberation.fr/
debats/2020/03/09/l-esclavage-c-est-fini-meme-pour-les-
femmes-de-chambre_1781112/, accessed January 9, 2020. See also
Justine Fontaine, "Au Chili, le slam qui blâme les violeurs,"
Libération, December 20, 2019, www.liberation.fr/
planete/2019/12/20/au-chili-le-slam-qui-blame-les-violeurs_
1770502/, accessed October 8, 2021.

43. Elsa Dorlin, "Les féminicides sont l'expression ultime d'un
continuum de pouvoir," *Les Inrocks*, December 31, 2019, www.
lesinrocks.com/2019/12/31/actualite/societe/2019-vue-par-
la-philosophe-elsa-dorlin-les-femicides-sont-lexpression-ultime-
dun-continuum-de-pouvoir/

44. See Zahra Ali, *Women and Gender in Iraq. Between Nation-Building
and Fragmentation* (Cambridge: Cambridge University Press,
2018).

45. Interview with Marc Pichaud, co-founder of Just Do IP, a firm
specializing in the question of video surveillance: "L'analyse des
risques conditionne le nombre de caméras et d'équipements,"
September 3, 2019, *infoprotection.fr*, in preparation for the APS
Fair, October 1–3, 2019. On the subject of the surveillance and
control market, see also, "Reportage à Milipol, le salon mondial de

la sécurité intérieure. Déclaration de guerre," December 9, 2019, *lundi.am*, https://lundi.am/Reportage-a-Milipol-le-salon-mondial-de-la-securite-interieure

46. "Aux grands hommes, le pays reconnaissant" (To the great men, the grateful homeland). Cécile Bouanchaud, "'Aux femmes assassinées, la patrie indifférente': Les 'colleuses' d'affiches veulent rendre visibles les victimes de fémicides," *Le Monde*, September 14, 2019, www.lemonde.fr/societe/article/2019/09/14/sur-les-murs-de-paris-des-collages-pour-denoncer-la-persistance-des-femicides_5510378_3224.html, accessed January 9, 2020.

47. In 1968, to end the widespread strike action that had brought France to a standstill, the government and trade unions signed agreements in rue de Grenelle, Paris. Ever since, "holding a Grenelle" signifies holding a public consultation on a major subject.

48. Virginie Baillet, "À Paris, la déferlante #NousToutes," *Libération*, November 24, 2019. See also www.lemonde.fr/societe/article/2019/11/24/a-paris-le-defile-contre-les-violences-faites-aux-femmes-en-images_6020314_3224.html

49. Lili B, "Féminisme made in Schiappa: Pot-pourri de réactionnaires à son Université d'été," *Révolution permanente*, September 4, 2018, www.revolutionpermanente.fr/Le-feminisme-made-in-Schiappa-pot-pourri-de-reactionnaires-a-son-Universite-d-ete; Hortense de Montalivet, "Raphaël Enthoven et son long monologue à l'université d'été du féminisme sont très mal passés," *HuffPost*, September 13, 2018, www.huffingtonpost.fr/entry/raphael-enthoven-et-son-long-monologue-a-luniversite-dete-du-feminisme-sont-tres-mal-passes_fr_5c92dc82e4b02a7e2d54158c

50. Police repression of the *Gilets Jaunes* (Yellow Vests) movement that emerged in November 2018 was particularly violent. In November 2019, journalist David Dufresne signaled 860 verified and documented cases of police violence during the Gilets Jaunes mobilizations from December 2018 to June 2019: hands blown off, demonstrators who lost an eye, or who were beaten following the many arrests and condemnations. See www.francetvinfo.fr/economie/transports/gilets-jaunes/gilets-jaunes-la-police-a-

blesse-en-quelques-mois-autant-de-manifestants-quen-vingt-ans_3702693.html. Previously, as this violence had long been inflicted particularly on racialized people, it did not make media headlines, nor was it the object of a national debate. But convergences between the *Gilet Jaunes* and racialized people fighting against police violence and its impunity helped highlight that violence and the systemic and structural nature of racism. The United Nations and the Council of Europe stated their concern at the excessive use of force in France and the limitations imposed on people's right to demonstrate peacefully.

51. In French: "Voici une classe qui se tient sage." Mattea Battaglia and Louise Couvelaire, "La vidéo de l'interpellation collective de dizaines de lycéens à Mantes-la-Jolie provoque de vives réactions," *Le Monde.fr*, December 6, 2018, www.lemonde.fr/police-justice/ article/2018/12/06/mantes-la-jolie-des-images-choquantes-de-lyceens-interpelles-par-la-police_5393757_1653578.html, accessed December 20, 2019.

52. Yessa Belkhodja, "Le 8 décembre nous marcherons contre la ségrégation et le racisme," *Contretemps*, November 8, 2019, www. contretemps.eu/mantois-police-segregation-racisme/, accessed December 21, 2019.

53. Geoffroy Clavel, "Jeunes arrêtés à Mantes-la-Jolie: Les réactions effarées des politiques. 'Images unacceptables', 'indigne de la République', 'intolérable', 'une jeunesse française humiliée'...," *Huffington Post*, December 7, 2018, www.huffingtonpost.fr/ entry/jeunes-arretes-a-mantes-la-jolie-les-reactions-effarees-des-politiques_fr_5c92b9dbe4b0ab349ef7533a, accessed January 5, 2020.

54. Ségolène Royal has had a very long parliamentary career in the Socialist Party. She was a minister in 2014–17, and ran for the Presidential election in 2007, where she was defeated in the run-off by Nicolas Sarkozy.

55. "Ségolène Royal sur les arrestations de Mantes-la-Jolie: 'Ca ne leur a pas fait de mal, à ces jeunes'," December 9, 2018, www. europe1.fr/politique/segolene-royal-sur-les-arrestations-de-mantes-la-jolie-ca-ne-leur-a-pas-fait-de-mal-a-ces-jeunes-3816953, accessed January 5, 2020.

56. "'Choquant', 'intolérable': les images de l'arrestation des 151 adolescents à Mantes-la-Jolie suscitent l'indignation à gauche. Les images montrent les jeunes alignés à genoux, les mains sur la tête, hier dans cette ville des Yvelines," December 7, 2018, www.francetvinfo.fr/faits-divers/police/choquant-intolerable-les-images-de-l-arrestation-des-151-lyceens-a-mantes-la-jolie-suscitent-l-indignation_3088939.html

57. Battaglia and Couvelaire, "La vidéo de l'interpellation collective de dizaines de lycéens … ."

58. Collectif des jeunes du Mantois, "Marche des mamans pour la justice et la dignité," *Mediapart*, September 3, 2019, *mediapart.fr*, https://blogs.mediapart.fr/collectif-de-defense-des-jeunes-du-mantois/blog/030919/marche-des-mamans-pour-la-justice-et-la-dignite, accessed December 20, 2019.

2 Race, Patriarchy, and the Politics of Women's Protection

1. Yvette Roudy, "Le scandale DSK est une affaire politique," *Le Monde*, June 28, 2011, www.lemonde.fr/idees/article/2011/06/28/le-scandale-dsk-est-une-affaire-politique_1542009_3232.html, accessed 21 December 2019.

2. The original French expression used was "*un troussage de domestique*," an old-fashioned term literally meaning "trussing the servants." David Doucet, "L'affaire DSK, 'un troussage de domestique'? Kahn s'excuse," *L'Express*, May 19, 2011, www.lexpress.fr/actualite/politique/l-affaire-dsk-un-troussage-de-domestique-kahn-s-excuse_994399.html, accessed 21 December 2019; "Affaire DSK: un 'troussage de domestique' pour Jean-François Khan," *Nouvel Obs*, May 19, 2011, www.nouvelobs.com/justice/l-affaire-dsk/20110519.OBS3497/affaire-dsk-un-troussage-de-domestique-pour-jean-francois-kahn.html, accessed 21 December 2019.

3. Alexandra Schwartzbrod and Laure Bretton, "Yvette Roudy, 'Nous sommes un pays de droits, de droits des hommes les biens nommés, comme je dis!'" *Libération*, December 13, 2019, www.liberation.fr/france/2013/12/13/yvette-roudy-nous-sommes-

un-pays-de-droits-de-droits-des-hommes-les-bien-nommes-comme-je-dis_966443, accessed 21 December 2019.

4. Emmanuel Macron, speech to the UN on September 25, 2019, cited on the website of the Secretary of State for Equality between Men and Women and the Fight Against Discrimination, www.egalite-femmes-hommes.gouv.fr/legalite-entre-les-femmes-et-les-hommes-priorite-du-g7/, accessed December 16, 2019.

5. Ibid.

6. Fati N'Zi Hassane, "La lutte contre l'excision doit s'intensifier en Afrique," *Le Monde Afrique*, August 13, 2019, www.lemonde.fr/afrique/article/2019/08/13/la-lutte-contre-l-excision-doit-s-intensifier-en-afrique_5499044_3212.html; see also: "Expériences de lutte contre l'excision en Afrique subsaharienne," www.genreenaction.net/Experiences-de-lutte-contre-l-excision-en-Afrique.html, which gives the dates of the organization on the continent of education programs by African women, and biographical references.

7. Press conference transcription, available on the Élysée website, August 25, 2019, www.elysee.fr/emmanuel-macron/2019/08/26/g7-biarritz-conference-de-presse-conjointe-consacree-au-program-afawa

8. Elsa Dorlin, "Macron, les femmes et l'Afrique: Un discours de sélection sexuelle et de triage colonial," *Le Monde*, November 30, 2017, www.lemonde.fr/afrique/article/2017/11/30/macron-les-femmes-et-l-afrique-un-discours-de-selection-sexuelle-et-de-triage-colonial_5222794_3212.html, accessed January 20, 2020. See also Françoise Vergès, "Macron et le ventre des femmes africaines, une idéologie misogyne et paternaliste," *L'Humanité*, July 17, 2017, www.humanite.fr/macron-et-le-ventre-des-femmes-africaines-une-ideologie-misogyne-et-paternaliste-638920

9. Ibid.

10. The OPIC was a development finance institution set up by the US government in 1971, advising North American companies on investing abroad. It merged with the Development Credit Authority (DCA) to form the US International Development Finance Corporation (DFC) in 2019.

11. "Les femmes et le microcrédit," *Babyloan*, www.babyloan.org/fr/les-femmes-et-le-microcredit

12. On this subject, see the work by historian Stephanie Jones-Rogers, *They Were Her Property. White Women as Slave Owners in the American South* (New Haven, CT: Yale University Press, 2019). Drawing on a rigorous study of the archives, the author shows that white women participated in the slave trade and slavery, from which they benefitted, that they were active advocates of the system, and that they successfully used it to gain social and economic status. Her study radically questions the feminist discourse of masculine domination, of patriarchy, by showing the links between slavery, capital, and gender. These white women accumulated wealth thanks to the system of white supremacy in which gender was not an obstacle.

13. See Kako Nubukpo, *L'Urgence africaine* (Paris: Odile Jacob, 2019); Dambisa Moyo, *L'Aide fatale* (Paris: Jean-Claude Lattès, 2009).

14. Coumba Kane, "Kako Nubukpo : "Le modèle de croissance des pays africains est mortifère," *Le Monde Afrique*, September 22, 2019, www.lemonde.fr/afrique/article/2019/09/22/kako-nubupko-le-modele-de-croissance-des-pays-africains-est-mortifere_6012608_3212.html

15. See *Le Point*, "Le 'décolonialisme', une stratégie hégémonique: l'appel de 80 intellectuels. Ils sont philosophes, historiens, professeurs ... Ils dénoncent des mouvances qui, sous couvert de lutte pour l'émancipation, réactivent l'idée de 'race'," November 28, 2018; Madinin'Art.net, "La pensée 'décoloniale' renforce le narcissisme des petites différences. 80 psychanalystes s'insurgent contre l'emprise croissante d'un dogme qui, selon eux, ignore la primauté du vécu personnel et dénie la spécificité de l'humain," September 25, 2019, www.madinin-art.net/la-pensee-decoloniale-renforce-le-narcissisme-des-petites-differences

16. Catherine Hall, "Mother Country," *London Review of Books*, January 23, 2020, 42(2), www.lrb.co.uk/the-paper/v42/no2/catherine-hall/mother-country, accessed February 1, 2020. Other publications include: Amelia Gentleman, *The Windrush Betrayal: Exposing the Hostile Environment* (London: Guardian Faber, 2019); Colin Grant, *Homecoming: Voices of the Windrush*

Generation (London: Cape, 2019), and Maya Goodfellow, *Hostile Environment: How Immigrants Become Scapegoats* (London: Verso, 2019).

17. Hall, "Mother Country."

18. Ibid. Edward Long, an eighteenth-century colonial administrator, slaveholder, and planter in Jamaica, wrote *History of Jamaica* (1774), which strongly influenced the debate on slavery in England. He opined that Black people were characterized by bestiality, stupidity, and degrading vices. *History of Jamaica* was republished by Cambridge University Press in 2010.

19. Ibid.

20. Jérémie Baruch, "Royaume-Uni: qu'est-ce que la génération Windrush?" *Le Monde*, April 30, 2018, www.lemonde.fr/les-decodeurs/article/2018/04/30/qu-est-ce-que-la-generation-windrush-qui-a-cause-la-demission-de-la-ministre-de-l-interieur-britannique_5292800_4355770.html; Kevin Rawlinson, "Windrush-era citizens row: Timeline of key events," *The Guardian*, April 16, 2018, www.theguardian.com/uk-news/2018/apr/16/windrush-era-citizens-row-timeline-of-key-events

21. See Hurard Bellance, *La Police des Noirs en Amérique (Martinique, Guadeloupe, Guyane, Saint-Domingue) et en France aux XVIIe et XVIIIe siècles* (Matoury: Ibis Rouge Editions, 2011).

22. Consular decree of May 1802 restoring slavery.

23. Louis N. Baudry Deslozières, *Les Égarements du Nigrophilisme* (Paris: Chez Migneret, 22 March 1802), p. 109. Dedicated to Joséphine de Beauharnais, the book is a long, negrophobic plea for the restoration of slavery and a review of the arguments that can still be heard today to diminish Europe's responsibility in the slave trade: slavery, it claimed, freed a continent plunged into war and tyranny from barbarity and savagery. Guided by their "bestiality" and natural laziness, Africans, it claimed, were incapable of understanding the meaning of freedom.

24. "Floréal" was the name of the eighth month of the revolutionary Republican calendar, abandoned on January 1, 1806.

25. Adet, cited in Antoine Claire Thibaudeau, *Mémoires Sur Le Consulat 1799–1804 (Par un Conseiller d'État)* (Paris: Libraire Chez Compieu et Cie, 1827), p. 210.

26. Text of Napoleon Bonaparte's decree, https://mjp.univ-perp.fr/france/1802esclavage.htm

27. *Bulletin des lois de la République française*, 3(219) (2001): 815–16.

28. Order pronounced by General Richepance restricting the title of citizen to white people alone, Basse-Terre, July 17, 1802, https://pyepimanla.blogspot.com/2019/07/arrete-du-general-richepance.html?m=0 (original emphasis).

29. Ibid.

30. See the remarkable chapter devoted to this period, "Last Days of Saint-Domingue," in Joan Dayan's *Haiti, History, and the Gods* (Berkeley: University of California Press, 1998).

31. Arlette Gautier, "Sous l'esclavage, le patriarcat," *Nouvelles Questions féministes*, 9/10(1985): 9–33. *JSTOR*, www.jstor.org/stable/40619392, accessed January 15, 2020.

32. Karen Bourdier, "Les conditions sanitaires sur les habitations sucrières de Saint-Domingue à la fin du siècle," *Dix-Huitième Siècle*, 43(1) (2011): 349–68.

33. Gautier, "Sous l'esclavage, le patriarcat," p. 13.

34. Jacqueline Jones, *Labor of Love, Labor of Sorrow: Black women, work, and the family, from slavery to the present* (New York: Basic Books, 1985).

35. Arlette Gautier, "Les esclaves femmes du Nouveau Monde," "Femmes et esclavage" colloquium, November 7–8, 2001, www.genreenaction.net/Les-esclaves-femmes-du-Nouveau-Monde-etude.html

36. Françoise Vergès, *Abolir l'esclavage: Une utopie coloniale. Les ambiguïtés d'une politique humanitaire* (Paris: Albin Michel, 2001).

37. Victor Schoelcher (1804–93) is considered in France to be the leading figure behind the definitive abolition of slavery in 1848 (decree of April 27, 1848). A Republican, an advocate of a "humanist" colonization, this eminent French abolitionist did not, however, oppose the financial compensation of slave owners. A recent CNRS publication revealed that the compensation granted from 1849 onwards to 10,000 slaveholders who filed a request totaled at 126 million gold francs (i.e., the equivalent today of 27 billion euros): www.lemonde.fr/afrique/article/2021/05/08/

les-compensations-versees-aux-proprietaires-d-esclaves-par-la-france-au-xixe-siecle-rendues-publiques_6079584_3212.html

38. See Francis Arzalier, "Les mutations de l'idéologie coloniale en France avant 1848: De l'esclavagisme à l'abolitionnisme," in Marcel Dorigny (ed.), *Les Abolitions de l'esclavage de L.F. Sonthonoax à V. Schoelcher* (Paris-Saint-Denis: Presses universitaires de Vincennes-Éditions UNESCO, 1995), pp. 301–8; Robin Blackburn, *The Overthrow of Colonial Slavery, 1776–1848* (London: Verso, 1988).

39. See Michèle Becquemin and Michel Chauvière, "L'enfance en danger: Genèse et évolution d'une politique de protectione," *Enfances & Psy*, 2013, 3(60): 16–27, www.cairn.info/revue-enfances-et-psy-2013-3-page-16.htm

40. Nadera Shalhoub-Kevorkian, *Incarcerated Childhood and the Politics of Unchilding* (Cambridge: Cambridge University Press, 2019), e-book. See also, Nadera Shalhoub-Kevorkian, *Militarization and Violence against Women in Conflict Zones in the Middle East: A Palestinian Case-Study* (Cambridge: Cambridge University Press, 2009); *Women and Political Conflict: The Case of Palestinian Women in Jerusalem* (Jerusalem: Women's Studies Center, 2006), and *Birthing in Occupied East Jerusalem: Palestinian Women's Experience of Pregnancy and Delivery* (Jerusalem: YWCA, 2012).

41. See Ivan Jablonka, *Enfants en exil, transfert de pupilles réunionnais en métropole (1963–1982)* (Paris: Seuil, 2007); Gilles Ascaride, Corine Spagnoli, and Philippe Vitale, *Tristes Tropiques de la Creuse* (Ile-sur-Têt: Éditions K'A, 2004); Jean-Jacques Martial, *Une enfance volée* (Paris: Les quatre chemins, 2003), and Jean-Pierre Gosse, *La Bête que j'ai été. Le témoignage d'un Réunionnais déporté dans la Creuse en 1966* (Céret: Editions Alter Ego, 2005).

42. "Pour Adel Benna, frère de Zyed, 'la France est devenue un cauchemar'," *20 minutes*, October 25, 2015, www.20minutes.fr/societe/1716475-20151025-adel-benna-frere-zyed-france-devenue-cauchemar

43. Ibid.

44. "Mineur ou majeur? Les tests osseux pour les jeunes migrants devant le Conseil constitutionnel," *La Croix*, March 12, 2019, www.la-croix.com/France/Mineur-majeur-tests-osseux-jeunes-migrants-devant-Conseil-constitutionnel-2019-03-12-

1301008264; Oriane Mollaret, "Mineurs isolés étrangers: les tests osseux en question," *Politis*, March 12, 2019, www.politis.fr/articles/2019/03/mineurs-isoles-etrangers-les-tests-osseux-en-question-40121/

45. Sylvia Wynter, https://globalsocialtheory.org/thinkers/wynter-sylvia/

46. Donna Haraway, "Anthropocene, Capitalocene, Plantationocene, Chthulucene: Making Kin," *Environmental Humanities*, 2015, 6: 159–65.

47. Ibid.

48. Ian Angus, Simon Butler, Betsy Hartmann and Joel Kovel (eds.), *Too Many People? Population, Immigration and the Environmental Crisis* (Chicago, IL: Haymarket Books, 2011).

49. Ibid.

50. Kalpana Wilson, "The new global population control policies: Fuelling India's sterilization atrocities," *Different Takes*, 2015, 87: 3, https://compass.fivecolleges.edu/object/hampshire:234

51. Ibid., p. 1.

52. Ibid.

53. Ibid., p. 3.

3 The Impasse of Punitive Feminism

1. Leila Ettachfini, "Mona Eltahawy would like you to fuck right off with your civility politics," *Vice*, December 27, 2019, www.vice.com/en_us/article/xgq8nz/mona-eltahawy-would-like-you-to-fuck-right-off-with-your-civility-politics, accessed January 20, 2020.

2. Elsa Dorlin, *Se défendre* (Paris: La Découverte, 2007).

3. Ibid.

4. Ibid.

5. Ettachfini, "Mona Eltahawy would like you to fuck right off with your civility politics."

6. Naomi Alderman, *The Power* (New York: Viking, 2016).

7. Dorlin, *Se défendre*, ebook emplacement 2949, and Elsa Dorlin, "Autodéfense et sécurité," https://tarage.noblogs.org/post/2020/04/02/autodefense-et-securite-elsa-dorlin/

8. Agnès Giard, "Pourquoi les femmes ont-elles peur dans la rue," *Libération*, January 6, 2020, http://sexes.blogs.liberation.fr/2020/01/06/pourquoi-les-femmes-ont-elles-peur-dans-la-rue/. Also see Titiou Lecoq, "Intimité et loup," in Muriel Flis-Trèves and René Frydman (eds.), *Intimités en danger* (Paris: PUF, hors collection, 2019).

9. See Valérie Rey-Robert, *Une culture du viol à la française* (Paris: Libertalia, 2019), and Noémie Richard and Michelle Perrot, *En finir avec la culture du viol* (Paris: Les petits matins, 2018).

10. Rey-Robert, *Une culture du viol*, p. 242.

11. Cited in ibid., p. 248.

12. Ibid.

13. UN-Women, "Facts and figures: Ending violence against women," 2016, www.unwomen.org/en/what-we-do/ending-violence-against-women/facts-and-figures

14. Ibid.

15. Kate Wilkinson, "Five facts: Femicide in South Africa," *Africa Check*, September 3, 2019—Wilkinson adds that fifty men are raped every day; and Thuso Khumalo, "South Africa declares femicide a national crisis", *Voanews*, September 20, 2019.

16. Ray Mwareya-Mhondera, "South Africa's brave struggle against lesbian hate crimes," March 3, 2015, https://wagingnonviolence.org/2015/03/south-africas-brave-struggle-against-lesbian-hate-crimes/; "Une pétition contre le viol des lesbiennes en Afrique du Sud," *Slate*, January 13, 2011.

17. Cathy Lafon, "Lutte contre les violences conjugales: l'Espagne pionnière en Europe," *Sud-Ouest*, March 16, 2019, www.sudouest.fr/2019/03/15/lutte-contre-les-violences-conjugales-l-espagne-pionniere-en-europe-5901659-5022.php, accessed December 16, 2019; "En Espagne, des milliers de personnes manifestent contre les violences faites aux femmes," *Le Monde*, September 21, 2019.

18. Lucas Robinson, "155 femicides in Argentina in first half of 2019," *Buenos Aires Times*, August 31, 2019.

19. Terre solidaire, "Dans le Brésil d'aujourd'hui, que signifie être une femme, être noire, et faire de l'agroécologie?" July 2, 2019, https://ccfd-terresolidaire.org/nos-publications/fdm/2019/309-juin-2019/dans-le-bresil-d-6391

20. Institut IFOP. See also: Richard and Perrot, *En finir avec la culture du viol*; Lauren Bastide, *Présentes* (Paris: Allary Éditions, 2020); the blog https://afrofem.com; "Femmes noires et violence sexuelle: visibilité et stigmatisation," policyoptions.irpp.org, https://policyoptions.irpp.org/magazines/march-2020/femmes-noires-et-violence-sexuelle-visibilite-et-stigmatisation/facebook-femmes-noires-et-violence-sexuelle-visibilite-et-stigmatisation/

21. Maya Finoh and Jasmine Sankofa, "Legal System has failed Black girls, women, and non-binary survivors of violence," *ACLU*, January 28, 2019, www.aclu.org/blog/racial-justice/race-and-criminal-justice/legal-system-has-failed-black-girls-women-and-non, accessed December 16, 2019.

22. Aubrey Hill, "Justice pour les femmes amérindiennes," Center for Health Progress, November 7, 2018, https://centerfor healthprogress.org/blog/justice-for-native-american-women/?g clid=CjoKCQiAz53vBRCpARIsAPPsz8WPAPH3aEfQWkP mPR6-yq9qKPLJG18mWxuTt327lZ5XTddCjDezv5UaAhoBE ALw_wcB, accessed December 16, 2019.

23. www.rtl.fr/actu/debats-societe/aux-etats-unis-les-femmes-noires-davantage-touchees-par-la-mortalite-maternelle-7792131375

24. Hill, "Justice pour les femmes amérindiennes."

25. Jennifer Brant, "Femmes et filles autochtones disparues et assassinées au Canada," *Encyclopédie canadienne*, July 5, 2019, www.thecanadianencyclopedia.ca/fr/article/missing-and-murdered-indigenous-women-and-girls-in-Canada, accessed December 16, 2019; Diane Poupeau, "Au Canada, des femmes autochtones sont tuées dans l'indifférence quasi générale," *Slate*, June 20, 2019; also see Kim O'Bomsawin's film, *Le Silence qui tue*, 2015–16.

26. "Poll ranks India the world's most dangerous country for women," *The Guardian*, June 28, 2018.

27. Le Monde.fr and AFP, "En Inde, des manifestations de colère après le viol et le meurtre d'une jeune femme," December 2, 2019, https://www.lemonde.fr/international/article/2019/12/02/en-inde-des-manifestations-de-colere-apres-le-viol-et-le-meurtre-

d-une-jeune-femme_6021382_3210.html, accessed December 19, 2019.

28. Ibid.

29. Le Monde and AFP, "Inde: quatre suspects du viol et du meurtre d'une femme abattus par la police lors d'une reconstitution," December 6, 2019, www.lemonde.fr/international/article/2019/12/06/inde-quatre-suspects-du-viol-et-du-meurtre-d-une-femme-abattus-par-la-police-lors-d-une-reconstitution_6021880_3210.html, accessed December 16, 2019.

30. UN-Women, "Facts and figures: Ending violence against Women," November 2018, www.unwomen.org/en/what-we-do/ending-violence-against-women/facts-and-figures, accessed December 16, 2019.

31. Observatoire des inégalités, "La pauvreté selon le sexe," September 26, 2017, www.inegalites.fr/La-pauvrete-selon-le-sexe?id_theme=22, accessed January 13, 2020. "Poverty does not affect men and women in the same way, according to the age group. Under the age of 18, the poverty rate of girls (taken as half the median household income and under) is equivalent to that of boys (11%). Children are affected in the same way by their parents' poverty. A gap widens between young adults ... Women are indeed more often at the head of a one-parent family than men with, as their only resources, benefits or a part-time salary. The gap is also considerable between older people: over 75 years old, the poverty rate of women is 3.4% (half the medium household income or lower) against 2.2% of men."

32. Jérôme Vincent, "Interview d'Octavia Butler,", *ActusF*, September 20, 2018, www.actusf.com/detail-d-un-article/interview-d-octavia-butler, accessed December 18, 2019. The interview was published in French; as no original English version is referenced, this English version of the citation has been translated from the French.

33. Ibid.

34. Andrea Hairston, "Octavia Butler – Praise song for a prophetic artist in Octavia Butler *Kindred*," *Melus*, 2001, 26: 293.

35. Ibid., p. 297.

36. Angelyn Mitchell, "Not enough of the past: Feminist revisions of slavery in Octavia Butler's *Kindred*," *Melus*, 2001, 26: 24, cited by Terryn Asunder, "Women, Community and Power in Octavia Butler's *Kindred*," *Anti-Imperialism.org*, August 26, 2011, https://anti-imperialism.org/2011/08/26/women-community-and-power-in-octavia-butlers-kindred/

37. See Lissell Quiroz and Rafik Chekkat, "Abolir le système pénal: entretien avec Gwenola Ricordeau (2ᵉ partie)", *État d'exception*, June 16, 2019, www.etatdexception.net/abolir-le-systeme-penal-entretien-avec-gwenola-ricordeau-2eme-partie/

38. Alex Press, "#MeToo doit éviter le féminisme carcéral," *Paris-Lutte Info*, November 21, 2019, https://paris-luttes.info/metoo-doit-eviter-le-feminisme-12656#nb17

39. Elizabeth Bernstein, "The sexual politics of the 'New Abolitionism'", *Differences*, 2007, 18(3): 128–51, p. 137.

40. Press, "#MeToo doit éviter le féminisme carcéral."

41. Éloïse Broch, Charlotte Dupeux, and Valentine Welter, "La prison n'est pas féministe,"! *lundi-matin*, December 4, 2017, https://lundi.am/La-prison-n-est-pas-feministe

42. La Ligue des droits des femmes in 1976, cited by Martine Le Péron, "Priorité aux violées," *Question féministes*, 1978, 3: 85.

43. In the interviews published by the monthly *Des femmes en mouvement* (#8–9, December 1978–January 1979), women imprisoned in Fleury Merogis (a notorious French prison, the largest in Europe) spoke of the difficulty of finding other forms of action than the hunger strike, to make themselves heard, saying that the "recourse to justice seems irremediable." Cited by Jean Bérard, "Dénoncer et (ne pas) punir les violences sexuelles? Luttes féministes et critiques de la répression en France de mai 68 au début des années 1980," *Politix*, 2014, 107(3): 61–84, p. 79.

44. Gwenola Ricordeau, *Pour elles toutes. Femmes contre la prison* (Paris: Lux, 2019), p. 146.

45. Nicolas Bourgoin, "Les automutilations et les grèves de la faim en prison," *Déviance et Société*, 2001/2, 25: 131–45, p. 134, www.cairn.info/revue-deviance-et-societe-2001-2-page-131.htm, DOI: 10.3917/ds.252.0131.

46. Jean-Claude Vimont, "Les emprisonnements des maoïstes et la détention politique en France (1970–1971)," *Criminocorpus* [Online], "Giustizia e detentzione politica, Le régime spécifique de la détention politique," published online October 6, 2015, http://journals.openedition.org/criminocorpus/3044, accessed January 28, 2020.

47. Ibid.

48. See Guillaume Attencourt's film, *La Petite Roquette* (2013), in which the director reconstitutes this fortress-like women's prison through the testimonies of former detainees, the female prison governor, educators, guards, nuns, and a wealth of archive images. There were both political prisoners—over 4,000 members of the Resistance during WWII; during the Algerian War, the Cold War, and post-May '68 demonstrations; the feminist Nadja Ringart was also imprisoned there—and common-law prisoners. The film reveals that the majority of detainees were women of modest condition, often incarcerated for minor offenses (bounced cheques, theft, etc.). The prison was pulled down in 1973–74.

49. A reference to October 17, 1961, when, on the orders of Prefect Papon, the French police arrested thousands of Algerians who were demonstrating peacefully against the curfew that had been imposed on them and threw them into the River Seine alive.

50. Françoise Picq, *Libération des femmes: les années-mouvement* (Paris: Seuil, 1993); also see Cathy Bernheim, *Perturbation, ma sœur. Naissance d'un mouvement de femmes* (Paris: Seuil, 1983).

51. René Pleven (1901–93), who was Minister of the Colonies and Finance and a life-long advocate of colonialism, was targeted here as the Minister of Justice (1969–73). It was indeed at this time that prison conditions in France began to be systematically denounced, and imprisoned extreme left-wing activists demanded the status of political prisoner and sought to join forces with common-law prisoners. Pleven staunchly opposed this movement, which was strengthened by the creation on February 8, 1971 of the *Groupe Information Prisons* (GIP), as announced by philosopher Michel Foucault during a press conference at the Chapelle Saint-Bernard. The prison revolts that broke out in 1971 and 1972 shed light on the inhuman conditions of French prisons: Vimont, "Les

emprisonnements des maoïstes et la détention politique en France (1970–1971)"; see also Fanny Bugnon, "La violence politique au prisme du genre à travers la presse française (1970–1994)," PhD thesis, Université d'Angers, 2011.

52. Vimont, "Les emprisonnements des maoïstes . . . ."

53. "Le Groupe Information sur les Prisons (GIP), 1971–1972," *Paris-Luttes-Info*, October 20, 2018, https://paris-luttes.info/le-groupe-d-information-sur-les, accessed January 20, 2020.

54. Simon Barbarit, citing Laurent Mucchielli, "Délinquance: des chiffres à la baisse mais le sentiment d'insécurité augmente," December 7, 2017, www.publicsenat.fr/article/politique/delinquance-des-chiffres-a-la-baisse-mais-le-sentiment-d-insecurite-augmente-80581. See also Laurent Mucchielli and Émilie Raquet, "Victimation et sentiment d'insécurité dans une petite ville de l'agglomération marseillaise," *Les Rapports de l'Observatoire de la délinquance*, 2017, no. 10, 2017, and Laurent Mucchielli's highly enlightening article on the evolution of normativity in the French judicial world, "L'impossible constitution d'une discipline criminologie en France: Cadres constitutionnels, enjeux normatifs et développements de la recherche des années 1880 à nos jours," *Criminologie*, 2004, 37(1): 13–42.

55. A child had just been found murdered.

56. Igor Martinache and Laurent Bonelli, "*La France a peur.* Une histoire sociale de 'l'insécurité'," *Lectures*, Minutes, 2008, posted online June 10, 2008, http://journals.openedition.org/lectures/611, accessed February 5, 2020. See also Laurent Bonelli, *La Machine à punir, Pratiques et discours sécuritaires* (Paris: L'Esprit frappeur, 2011); Nicolas Bourgoin, *La République contre les libertés – Le virage autoritaire de la gauche libérale (1995–2014)* (Paris: L'Harmattan, 2015); Laurent Mucchielli, *La Frénésie sécuritaire. Retour à l'ordre et nouveau contrôle social* (Paris: La Découverte, 2008); idem, "Le développement de l'idéologie sécuritaire et ses conséquences en France des années 1970 à nos jours," *Regards croisés sur l'économie* 2017, 1(20): 111–21, and *Violences et insécurité. Fantasmes et réalités dans le débat français* (Paris: La Découverte, 2001).

57. www.laurent-mucchielli.org/index.php?pages/Sociologie-de-la-delinquance

58. *Histoire d'elles*, 2, 1977; see also Jean Bérard, "Dénoncer et (ne pas) punir les violences sexuelles? Luttes féministes et critiques de la répression en France de mai 68 au début des années 1980," *Politix*, 2014, 3(107): 61–84, https://www.cairn.info/revue-politix-2014-3-page-61.htm

59. *Le Quotidien des femmes*, June 25, 1976.

60. Odile Dhavernas, *Droits des femmes, pouvoir des hommes* (Paris: Seuil, 1978), pp. 375–80.

61. Founded in 1971, the FHAR was rapidly criticized by lesbians then racialized women. On the racialized and queer movement, see "Du Fhar aux collectifs trans, intersexes, queers et racisés, 50 ans de mobilisation associative LGBT+ en France," *KOMITID*, June 28 2019, www.komitid.fr/2019/06/28/du-fhar-aux-collectifs-trans-intersexes-queers-et-racises-50-ans-de-mobilisation-associative-lgbt-en-france/ and "En Marge des Fiertés, c'est un espace par et pour les personnes queers et racisées," *KOMITID*, June 21, 2018, www.komitid.fr/2018/06/21/en-marge-des-fiertes-espace-queer-racise-lyon/

62. Françoise d'Eaubonne, "Affaire Azuelos: Merci monsieur le procureur. Pour une réponse pratique à la question du viol," *Les Cahiers du Grif*, 1976, 14–15: 72–6, p. 75, www.persee.fr/doc/grif_0770-6081_1976_num_14_1_1131

63. Ibid.

64. *Des femmes en mouvement*, December 1978–January 1979, no. 12–13.

65. *Cahiers du féminisme*, 1980, no. 14.

66. Gisèle Halimi (1927–2020) was a feminist, lawyer, and politician. She defended the members of the Algerian National Liberation Front (FLN), but it was her defense of the young Algerian militant Djamila Boupacha, tortured and raped by French parachutists, that brought her to the public eye. In 1971, she founded the *Choisir* (Choose) movement, defended women accused of illegal abortion in 1972 during the famous Bobigny trial that contributed to the passing of the 1975 Veil Law legalizing abortion, and that in 1978

of two women rape victims which contributed to the adoption of a new law on rape in France in 1980. She later became a Socialist Party MP and held positions at UNESCO and the UN.

67. *Choisir*, 1980, no. 48.

68. *Des femmes en mouvement*, December 1978–January 1979, no.12–13.

69. The law legalizing abortion was voted in in 1978, and in 1996 a new law was voted in concerning rape.

70. Librairie des femmes de Milan, *Ne crois pas avoir des droits* (Bordeaux: Editions la Tempête, 2019), p. 116.

71. Ibid.

72. Ibid., p. 121.

73. Ibid.

74. Ibid., p. 120.

75. Ibid.

76. Lilian Mathieu, "Prostituées et féministes en 1975 et 2002: l'impossible reconduction d'une alliance,", *Travail, genre et sociétés*, 2003, 2(10): 31–48, p. 33, www.cairn.info/revue-travail-genre-et-societes-2003-2-page-31.htm; see also Christine Machiels, *Les Féministes et la prostitution (1860–1960)* (Rennes: Presses universitaires de Rennes, 2016).

77. Mathieu, "Prostituées et féministes en 1975 et 2002 ... ," p. 34.

78. Ibid.

79. Lilian Mathieu, *La Fin du tapin. Sociologie de la croisade pour l'abolition de la prostitution* (Paris: F. Bourin, 2014), cited by Alban Jacquemart and Milena Jakšić, "Droits des femmes ou femmes sans droits? Le féminisme d'État face à la prostitution," *Genre, sexualité & société*, Autumn 2018, no. 20, published online January 1, 2019, http://journals.openedition.org/gss/5006; DOI: 10.4000/gss.5006, accessed 27 January 2020.

80. Yolande Cohen, "De parias à victimes. Mobilisations féministes sur la prostitution en France et au Canada (1880–1920)," *Genre, sexualité & société*, Spring 2014, no. 11, published online July 1, 2014, accessed February 11, 2020.

81. Ibid.

82. Jacquemart and Jakšić, "Droits des femmes ou femmes sans droits? ... ."

83. Ibid.
84. Ibid.
85. Ibid.
86. "Nos 30 arguments en faveur de l'abolition de la prostitution," April 2014, www.mouvementdunid.org/Nos-30-arguments-en-faveur-de-l-abolition-de-la-prostitution, accessed December 19, 2019.
87. Jacquemart and Jakšić, "Droits des femmes ou femmes sans droits? . . . ."
88. Cited in ibid.
89. See Sabrina Sánchez, "Remasculinización del Estado y precariedad feminizada," in *Violencias, Racismo y Colonialidad* (Barcelona: Desde El Margen, 2017), pp. 179–82, p. 182. See the arguments of the *Nid pour l'abolition* movement, www.mouvementdunid.org/Nos-30-arguments-en-faveur-de-l-abolition-de-la-prostitution
90. See "Ni abolitionnistes, ni réglementaristes: syndicalistes!", http://strass-syndicat.org/le-strass/nos-revendications/ni-abo-ni-reglo-syndicalistes/
91. Lilian Mathieu, "Prostituées et féministes en 1975 et 2002 ... ," p. 34.
92. Ibid., p. 35.
93. For more on this subject, see Miriam Ticktin's enlightening analysis, "Sexual violence as the language of border control: Where French feminist and anti-immigrant rhetoric meet," *Signs, Journal of Women in Culture and Society*, 2008, 33(4): 863–89.
94. Valencia, *Gore Capitalism*.
95. For more on this evolution, see Brenna Bhandar and Rafeef Ziadah (eds.), *Revolutionary Feminisms* (London: Verso, 2020), a compilation of interviews with revolutionary, radically anti-racist, anti-imperialist, anti-capitalist feminists, who root their theoretical reflection and their praxis in a historicity of struggles.
96. Kim Hullot-Guiot and Leila Piazza, "Abolir la prostitution? Les féministes applaudissent, les prostituées moins," *Libération*, June 25, 2012, www.liberation.fr/societe/2012/06/25/abolir-la-prostitution-les-feministes-applaudissent-les-prostituees-moins_828945
97. Ibid.

98. Ibid.

99. Lilian Mathieu, "Prostituées et féministes en 1975 et 2002 ... ," p. 47.

100. Jacquemart and Jakšić, "Droits des femmes ou femmes sans droits? ... ."

101. Miriam Ticktin, "Sexual Violence as the language of border control ... ," p. 871.

102. *La Croix*, November 6, 2009, https://www.la-croix.com/Archives/2009-11-06/Yvette-Roudy-La-burqa-c-est-une-histoire-de-domination-organisee.-On-gomme-l-identite-des-femmes-.-C-est-un-engrenage-il-faut-une-loi.-_NP_-2009-11-06-357347

103. Anne Vigerie and Anne Zelensky, "Laïcardes, puisque féministes," *Le Monde*, May 29, 2003, www.lemonde.fr/archives/article/2003/05/29/laicardes-puisque-feministes-par-anne-vigerie-et-anne-zelensky_321962_1819218.html, accessed December 21, 2019 (original emphasis).

104. On this subject, see Chandra Talpande Mohanty's text, "Under Western eyes: Feminist scholarship and colonial discourses," *Feminist Review*, 1988, 30: 61–88, which remains a fundamental reference.

105. The *Comité Laïcité République* website lists 15 articles in national newspapers between 2016 and 2018, www.laicite-republique.org/-cafes-interdits-aux-femmes.html. Laurent Mucchielli counted 18 articles in *Le Monde* on the subject of neighborhood gang rapes between 2000 and 2001; see Laurent Mucchielli, *Le Scandale des "tournantes": Dérives médiatiques, contre-enquête sociologique* (Paris: La Découverte, 2005).

106. Ibid., p. 22.

107. Title of the weekly newspaper *Marianne*, January 5–11, 1998, cited by Linda Saadoui, "Laurent Mucchielli, *Le Scandale des 'tournantes'. Dérives médiatiques, contre-enquête sociologique*," *Questions de communication* 2006, no. 19, https://journals.openedition.org/questionsdecommunication/7788?lang=en#authors, accessed December 22, 2019.

108. Saadoui, "Laurent Mucchielli ... ."

109. Ibid.

110. While France's *banlieues*, or suburbs, are home to all socioeconomic categories, and made up of all types of housing and residential neighborhoods, the term is often understood to refer specifically to its predominantly racialized, working-class high-density housing projects.

111. Claire Cosquer, "La "société" contre la 'Cité'. La construction des tournantes comme problème racial," Sciences Po, *Observatoire sociologique du changement*, April 2015, 3 : 22.

112. Nadia Remadna, "Un café interdit aux femmes en France en 2016 ? Oui, c'est la faute des pouvoirs publics," *L'Obs. Le Plus*, December 9, 2016, http://leplus.nouvelobs.com/contribution/1631032-un-cafe-interdit-aux-femmes-en-france-en-2016-oui-c-est-la-faute-des-pouvoirs-publics.html

113. Xavier Frison, "Des cafés interdits aux femmes en France ? Benoît Hamon relativise ... ," *Marianne*, December 18, 2016, www.marianne.net/politique/des-cafes-interdits-aux-femmes-en-france-benoit-hamon-relativisechap 4 feminisme carceral 6_02.d

114. Ibid. An Arabic loanword, *bled* designates the home country.

115. Louise Hermant, "'Cafés interdits aux femmes à Sevran': un responsable de France Télé reconnaît un bug," *Les Inrocks*, February 9, 2018, www.lesinrocks.com/2018/02/09/medias-actualite/medias-actualite/cafe-interdit-aux-femmes-sevran-un-responsable-de-france-tele-reconnait-un-bug/

116. The *Bondy Blog* is an "online media born at the time of the November 2005 urban revolts that followed the death of Zyed Benna and Bouna Traoré. It was founded by the Swiss magazine *L'Hebdo* in the aim of giving the inhabitants of working-class neighborhoods a voice," www.bondyblog.fr/qui-sommes-nous/

117. Ibid.

118. https://npns.eu/, accessed December 21, 2019.

119. Angela Davis, *Abolition Democracy. Beyond Empire, Prisons and Torture* (New York: Seven Stories Press, 2005), p. 65.

120. "En soutien aux meufs trans incarcérées et pour un féminisme contre les prisons," January 30, 2020, https://paris-luttes.info/en-soutien-aux-meufs-trans-13425

121. Ibid.

122. Ibid.

123. Laure Anelli, "Les femmes épargnées par la justice?" *Observatoire international des prisons, Section française*, January 28, 2020, https://oip.org/analyse/les-femmes-epargnees-par-la-justice/

124. Laure Anelli, "Femmes détenues: les oubliées," *Dedans-Dehors*, December 2019, no. 106; *Observatoire international des prisons, Section française*, https://oip.org/publication/femmes-detenues/

125. Ibid.

126. Corinne Rostaing, cited in ibid.

127. Ibid.

128. Jacques Lesage de La Haye, cited by Grégory Salle, *L'Utopie carcérale. Petite histoire des «prisons modèles»* (Paris: Éditions Amsterdam, 2016), p. 192.

129. Gwenola Ricordeau, *Les Détenus et leurs proches. Solidarités et sentiments à l'ombre des murs* (Paris: Autrement, 2008), p. 14.

130. Ibid., p. 197.

131. Michelle Perrot, *Les Ombres de l'histoire. Crimes et châtiments au XIXᵉ siècle* (Paris: Flammarion, 2001), p. 22.

132. "Angela Davis on prison abolition, the war on drugs and why social movements shouldn't wait on Obama," *Democracy Now*, March 6, 2011, www.democracynow.org/2014/3/6/angela_davis_on_prison_abolition_the, accessed December 21, 2019.

133. Salle, *L'Utopie carcérale* …, p. 196.

134. Quiroz and Chekkat, "Abolir le système pénal… ."

135. Ibid.

136. Ricordeau, *Pour elles toutes. Femmes contre la prison*, p. 153.

137. Victoria Law, "Against carceral feminism," *Jacobin*, October 17, 2014, www.jacobinmag.com/2014/10/against-carceral-feminism/, accessed December 21, 2019.

Conclusion: For a Decolonial Feminist Politics

1. The French government declared a "national health emergency" on March 17, 2020.

2. "Amazon Guardian, indigenous land defender, shot dead in Brazil," April 1, 2020, www.survivalinternational.org/news/12365

3. See the differences in contamination and death rates between Greece and France, between Taiwan, South Korea, Vietnam and the United States ... .

4. Nathalie Mayer, "La pollution de l'air est le fléau qui réduit le plus l'espérance de vie dans le monde," *Futura Santé*, March 8, 2020, www.futura-sciences.com/sante/actualites/vie-pollution-air-fleau-reduit-plus-esperance-vie-monde-63256/; also see Jos Lelieveld, Klaus Klingmüller, Andrea Pozzer, Ulrich Pöschl, Mohammed Fnais, Andreas Daiber, Thomas Münzel, "Cardiovascular disease burden from ambient air pollution in Europe reassessed using novel hazard ratio functions," *European Heart Journal*, May 4, 2019, 40(20): 1590–96, https://doi.org/10.1093/eurheartj/ehz135; Seong Rae Kim, Seulggie Choi, Kyuwoong Kim, Jooyoung Chang, Sung Min Kim, Yoosun Cho, Yun Hwan Oh, Gyeongsil Lee, Joung Sik Son, Kyae Hyung Kim, Sang Min Park, "Association of the combined effects of air pollution and changes in physical activity with cardiovascular disease in young adults," European Heart Journal, July 1, 2021, 42(25): 2487–97, https://doi.org/10.1093/eurheartj/ehab139; Michael Brauer, Barbara Casadei, Robert A Harrington, Richard Kovacs, Karen Sliwa, the WHF Air Pollution Expert Group, "Taking a stand against air pollution – the impact on cardiovascular disease: A Joint Opinion from the World Heart Federation, American College of Cardiology, American Heart Association, and the European Society of Cardiology," European Heart Journal, April 14, 2021, 42(15): 1460–63, https://doi.org/10.1093/eurheartj/ehaa1025

5. In the words of the *Jeunesse autochtone de Guyane* (JAG, Guiana Indigenous Youth) cited by Goldoracle, QuedlaGold, and Goldebois, *Ni or ni maître. Montagne d'or et consorts* (Les Editions du Couac, 2019), p. 20.

6. Charles Mills uses this term to designate what is written in invisible ink in the social contract, the tacit agreement between members of a white society: that the rules of the contract do not apply to the racialized. See Charles Mills, *The Racial Contract* (London: Cornell University Press, 1997).

7. "Kids, burn it down, burn it down! / Burn it down to bring order / Burn it down, bring disorder / Bring disorder to bring order": slogans chanted by Martiniquan feminists, in Florence Lazar's film, *Tu crois que la terre est morte / You Think the Earth is a Dead Thing*, 2019.

8. Ibid.

9. *Cancion sin miedo*, Mon Laferte, Vivir Quintana and the El Palomar choir (Song Without Fear), March 8, 2020, Mexico City, https://youtube/-UgyLRjz3Oc; the lyrics were written by Mon Laferte, in homage to a friend, victim of femicide.

10. Naomi Klein, "How Big Tech Plans to Profit from the Pandemic," *The Guardian*, May 13, 2020, www.theguardian.com/news/2020/may/13/naomi-klein-how-big-tech-plans-to-profit-from-coronavirus-pandemic?CMP=Share_iOSApp_Other

11. Nadine Fadel, "Pénurie d'eau en pleine crise de coronavirus: le préfet prend la main dans 6 communes de Guadeloupe," *Guadeloupe 1ʳᵉ*, March 19, 2020, https://la1ere.francetvinfo.fr/guadeloupe/penurie-eau-pleine-crise-coronavirus-prefet-prend-main-6-communes-guadeloupe-814152.html; in La Désirade, the same problem: en http://www.guadeloupe.gouv.fr/layout/set/print/Politiques-publiques/Risques-naturels-technologiques-et-sanitaires/Securite-sanitaire/Informations-coronavirus/L-eau/Distribution-de-bouteilles-d-eau-a-la-Desirade-vendredi-8-et-mardi-12-mai-de-8h-a-12h; and in Mayotte, Sophie Chapelle, "À Mayotte, 'avec le coronavirus, la dengue et la faim, le cocktail est explosif'," *Basta!*, April 29, 2020, www.bastamag.net/Mayotte-faim-pauvrete-acces-eau-penurie-petrole-maladie-chronique-epidemie-dengue-coronavirus-covid19, and Patrick Roger, "Coronavirus: à Mayotte, 'c'est impossible de rester à l'intérieur'," *Le Monde*, April 7, 2020, www.lemonde.fr/politique/article/2020/04/07/coronavirus-a-mayotte-c-est-impossible-de-rester-a-l-interieur_6035837_823448.html

12. The strike began on July 17, 2019. In May 2021, after a 22-month struggle, the Hotel Ibis Batignolle cleaning women won their fight and their demands were accepted by the Accor Hotel Group. Their denunciation of subcontracting has opened a new field of struggle.

13. *AJ+ France* Sur le terrain, "Ils pensent que nous sommes leurs esclaves et y'a pas de respect," February 19, 2020, www.facebook. com/watch/?v=1289267697931150

14. The status of the enslaved as objects was not exclusive to Western slavery. See, on this subject, James C. Scott, *Homo Domesticus. Une histoire profonde des premiers États* (Paris: La Découverte, 2019), who reveals that in Sumerian ledgers, the enslaved were recorded along with cattle or furniture. See also Paulin Ismard, *La Cité et ses esclaves. Institution, fictions, expériences* (Paris: Seuil, 2019). In the cases studied by the authors, there was no racialization equivalent to that of colonial slavery.

15. This is what Hortense Spillers explains in "Mama's baby Papa's maybe: An American grammar book," *Diacritics*, Summer 1987, pp. 65–81. See also Jones-Rogers, *They Were Her Property. White Women as Slave Owners in the American South.*

16. The linguist Gilles Guilleron, cited in "Mais pourquoi les jeunes des cités ont-ils un accent?" *Le Parisien*, November 27, 2017, www.leparisien.fr/archives/mais-pourquoi-les-jeunes-des-cites-ont-ils-un-accent-27-11-2012-2358671.php

17. In addition to H. Spiller's already-cited classic text, "Mama's Baby," see Thelma Golden (ed.), *Black Male. Representations of Masculinity in Contemporary American Art* (New York: Whitney Museum of American Art, 1994); English-language works on Black masculinity have multiplied over the last few years; a veritable theoretical corpus has developed, including in the arts.

18. The term was coined by feminist Moya Bailey in *They aren't talking about me*, March 14, 2010, www.crunkfeministcollective. com/2010/03/14/they-arent-talking-about-me/; also see: the *Mrs Roots* blog, *The Gradient Lair* blog, and the *Mwasi Collective* blog.

19. Philip Mirowski, *Never Let a Serious Crisis Go to Waste. How Neoliberalism Survived the Financial Meltdown* (London: Verso, 2013).

20. See Wendy Brown, *Edgework. Critical Essays on Knowledge and Politics* (Princeton, NJ: Princeton University Press, 2005), p. 40.

21. Mirowski, *Never Let a Serious Crisis Go to Waste* ... .

22. Its roll-out in French universities during the pandemic was clearly described by the *Quadrature du Net* in "Crise sanitaire: la technopolice envahit l'université," *La Quadrature du Net*, April 30, 2020, www.laquadrature.net/2020/04/30/crise-sanitaire-la-technopolice-envahit-luniversite/

23. Jean-Philippe Luis, "Coronavirus: la fortune de Jeff Bezos gonfle durant la pandémie," *Les Échos*, April 16, 2020, www.lesechos.fr/industrie-services/conso-distribution/coronavirus-la-fortune-de-jeff-bezos-gonfle-durant-la-pandemie-1195348; "Jeff Bezos s'est enrichi avec la pandémie contrairement aux autres ultra-riches', *Business Insider*, April 1, 2020, www.businessinsider.fr/jeff-bezos-sest-enrichi-avec-la-pandemie-contrairement-aux-autres-ultra-riches-184216

24. Ibid. From January 1 to April 10, 2020, the richest billionaires in the United States saw their fortunes increase by several tens of millions of dollars. See "Durant la pandémie, la fortune des milliardaires étatsuniens a augmenté de 282 milliards de dollars," *Reporterre*, May 2, 2020, https://reporterre.net/Durant-la-pandemie-la-fortune-des-milliardaires-etatsuniens-a-augmente-de-282-milliards

25. William I. Robinson, "Beyond the economic chaos of coronavirus is a global war economy", *Truthout*, March 23, 2020, https://truthout.org/articles/beyond-the-economic-chaos-of-coronavirus-is-a-global-war-economy/

26. Ibid.

27. Thomas Jusquiame, "Reportage à Milipol, le salon de la sécurité intérieure," *lundi.am*, December 9, 2019, https://lundi.am/Reportage-a-Milipol-le-salon-mondial-de-la-securite-interieure

28. Émilie Massemin and Isabelle Rimbert, "Nous avons visité Milipol, le salon de la répression," November 21, 2019, *Reporterre*, https://reporterre.net/Nous-avons-visite-Milipol-le-salon-de-la-repression

29. For example, the "we" in the French Prime Minister Edouard Philippe's declaration before the National Assembly on April 28, 2020: "We are going to have to live with the virus," www.rtl.fr/actu/politique/coronavirus-nous-allons-devoir-vivre-avec-le-virus-declare-edouard-philippe-7800453463

30. Robinson, "Beyond the economic chaos of coronavirus... ."

31. "Au nom de la lutte contre le coronavirus, la police française a déjà tué 5 personnes et fait plus de dix blessé graves," *Paris-Luttes.Info*, April 20, 2020, https://paris-luttes.info/au-nom-de-la-lutte-contre-le-covid-13848

32. Emmanuel Fansten, "Confinement: en Seine-Saint-Denis, un taux de verbalisation trois fois plus important qu'ailleurs," *Libération*, April 26, 2020.

33. "Violences policières et confinement: sept plaintes déposées. Les familles montent au créneau," *Révolution permanente*, April 20, 2020, https://revolutionpermanente.fr/Violences-policieres-et-confinement-7-plaintes-deposees-Les-familles-montent-au-creneau?fbclid=IwAR0LDDpUAjeWXBapZA4ootdUbOgH89Z_91Zyvimc3NfaAu5XjfgHJD4BvA; see also José Rostier, "Violences policières dans les quartiers: rien de neuf sous le Covid-19?," April 25, 2020, https://npa2009.org/actualite/jeunesse/violences-policieres-dans-les-quartiers-rien-de-neuf-sous-le-covid-19

34. *Bicot* (1892) is a derivative of *arbi*, or Arab, and is a racist slang term to describe North Africans: Olivier Bureau and Jean-Michel Décugis, "'Un bicot ça ne nage pas': deux policiers des Hauts-de-Seine suspendus après les propos racistes," *Le Parisien*, April 27, 2020, www.leparisien.fr/hauts-de-seine-92/deux-policiers-des-hauts-de-seine-suspendus-apres-s-etre-denonces-pour-des-propos-racistes-a-l-ile-saint-denis-27-04-2020-8306988.php

35. On October 17, 1961, a peaceful march was held to denounce the curfew that had just been applied only to the Maghrebi population in France, and to support the Algerian independence struggle. Maurice Papon, the Prefect of Paris—who, when he was Prefect of Bordeaux under the German Occupation, authorized the deportation of Jews to the death camps—gave his troops the order to harshly repress the march. The demonstrators were arrested in their hundreds. Some were thrown into the River Seine after being beaten, where they drowned. The youngest victim, Fetima Beddar, was 17 years old. The next day, Maurice Papon published a press release in which he minimized the repression (officially mentioning three deaths) and accused the demonstrators of violence against the police. Silence reigned, and it was only in the

1980s that historians began to publish research about the march and its repression. It was not until Maurice Papon's trial in 1997 for his anti-Semitic acts during the Occupation that the October 17 events publicly resurfaced.

36. Sonia Dayan-Herzbrun, "Une vie qui n'en est pas une," published in Spanish in the online journal *Comparative Cultural Studies*, May 12, 2020, and in French on the author's Facebook page.

37. "Pas sans Nous" Tribune, "Dans les quartiers populaires, imaginer le 'monde d'après', n'en déplaise aux plus sincères, reste un luxe," *Basta!*, May 5, 2020, www.bastamag.net/quartiers-populaires-detresse-economique-sociale-crise-stigmatisation-politique-d-exception-pouvoir-d-agir-habitants-associations

38. Tom Phillips, "'This is our feminist spring': Millions of Mexican women prepare to strike over femicides," *The Guardian*, March 7, 2020, www.theguardian.com/world/2020/mar/07/mexico-femicides-protest-women-strike

39. In Russia, for example, under the pressure of the Orthodox Church, a 2017 law was voted, which transformed the violence committed by a husband, partner, or father into "a family issue." Unless the victim is hospitalized, it is not considered a crime. Margarita Gracheva pressed charges against her husband in vain; the police did nothing. He ended up cutting off her hands: www.bbc.com/news/world-europe-49318003

40. On the myth of speaking out, see: https://paris-luttes.info/apres-metoo-comment-est-ce-13578, March 7, 2020.

41. Anthony Berthelier, "Marlène Schiappa a été 'choquée' par les images de la marche des femmes, mais ... ," *HuffPost*, March 8, 2020. www.huffingtonpost.fr/entry/marlene-schiappa-images-marche-femmes_fr_5e653a93c5b6670e72f9cc64

42. Johanna Brenner and Maria Ramas, "Repenser l'oppression des femmes. Capitalisme, reproduction biologique, travail industriel, structures familiales, État-providence. Un débat avec Michèle Barrett," March 1, 1984, www.europe-solidaire.org/spip.php?article38678

43. Angela Davis, "The color of violence against women. Keynote address at the Color of Violence Conference in Santa Cruz,"

Colorlines, Fall 2000, 3(3), www.colorlines.com/articles/color-violence-against-women

44. In books, manifestos, and artistic interventions, Black and Indigenous feminists have constructed a theory of revolutionary love, insisting on its force as a political practice. In the 1980s, see Cherrie Moraga and Gloria Anzaldua (eds.), *This Bridge Called My Back: Writings by Radical Women of Colour* (Watertown, MA: Persephone Press), 1981); Gloria Hull, Patricia Bell Scott and Barbara Smith (eds.), *All the Women Are White, All the Blacks Are Men, but Some of Us Are Brave: Black Women's Studies* (New York: Feminist Press, 1982); more recently, Jennifer Nash, "Practicing Love: Black Feminism, Love-Politics, and Post-Intersectionality," *Meridians*, 2011, 11(2): 1–24, and Kei Day, *Religious Resistance to Neoliberalism* (New York: Palgrave Macmillan, 2016), and notably the chapter, "Love as a Concrete Revolutionary Practice," pp. 105–29. In France, it was Houria Bouteldja's book, *Les Blancs, les Juifs et nous. Vers une politique de l'amour révolutionnaire* (Paris: La Fabrique, 2016; translated into English as *Whites, Jews, and Us. Toward a Politics of Revolutionary Love*) that introduced this concept into the political debate.

45. Aurélie Arnaud, "Féminisme autochtone militant: Quel féminisme pour quelle militance?" *Nouvelles Pratiques Sociales*, 2014, 27(1): 211–22.

46. Achille Mbembe, *Brutalisme* (Paris: La Découverte, 2020).

47. See the studies of the criminalization of childhood in Palestine, on the fact that Black girls and boys are always perceived and judged as older than they are by the police and justice system in the United States, and, remaining in the sphere of the French Republic, on the treatment of Roma, migrant, and refugee children (unaccompanied minors) in Mayotte or Réunion.

48. "'This is our everyday Mexico': Brutal murders of women and girl fuel mass protests," February 21, 2020, www.cbc.ca/radio/asithappens/as-it-happens-friday-edition-1.5471399/this-is-our-everyday-mexico-brutal-murders-of-woman-and-girl-fuel-mass-protests-1.5471867; "International Women's Day: Clashes mar Mexico City march," March 9, 2020, www.bbc.com/news/world-latin-america-51796605

49. *Libération*, March 8, 2020, www.liberation.fr/checknews/ 2020/03/08/que-sait-on-de-l-intervention-policiere-lors-de-la-manifestation-feministe-nocturne-a-paris_1780961

50. Syrine Attia, "Front-line activists 'Primera Linea' protect Chile's protesters, but some criticize their methods," *France 24*, March 1, 2020, https://observers.france24.com/en/20200103-frontline-activists-primera-linea-protecting-protesters-chile-santiago-super-heroes

51. David R. Roediger, *The Wages of Whiteness: Race and the Making of the American Working Class* (London and New York: Verso, 1991, revised edition 2007, with an introduction by Kathleen Cleaver). The cover description on the French version of the book states: "Both a system of real privileges and illusion appropriated by poor white people, upheld by the dominant classes, the 'wages of whiteness', continue to structure racial and economic domination in the United States." For France, see Rafik Chekkat and Emmanuel Delgado Hoch, *Race rebelle* (Paris: Syllepse, 2011), and Félix Boggio Éwanjé-Épée and Stella Magliani-Belkacem (eds.), *Race et Capitalisme* (Paris: Syllepse, 2012).

52. Fusco, *Petit manuel de torture à l'usage des femmes soldats*, p. 95.

53. Two examples: Johanna Brenner and Maria Ramas have shown that European laws to protect women in the workplace have not mitigated the gendered division of labor. See Brenner and Ramas, "Repenser l'oppression des femmes ... ", and Hicham Houdaïfa, *Dos de femme, dos de mulet. Les oubliées du Maroc profond* (Casablanca: En toutes lettres, 2015) and Chadia Arab, *Dames de fraises, doigts de fée. Les invisibles de la migration saisonnière marocaine en Espagne* (Casablanca: En toutes lettres, 2018) highlight the entanglement of oppressions, which are not reduced by progressive laws on women's rights.

54. On the violence/non-violence debate, see Starhawk, *Webs of Power: Notes from the Global Uprising* (Gabriola Island, BC, Canada: New Society Publishers, 2002), and Peter Gelderloos, *Comment la non-violence protège l'État. Essai sur l'inefficacité des mouvements sociaux* (Montréal: Éditions Libre, 2018).

Index

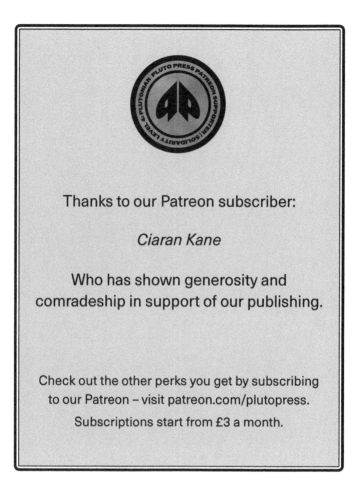

Thanks to our Patreon subscriber:

Ciaran Kane

Who has shown generosity and
comradeship in support of our publishing.

Check out the other perks you get by subscribing
to our Patreon – visit patreon.com/plutopress.

Subscriptions start from £3 a month.

The Pluto Press Newsletter

Hello friend of Pluto!

Want to stay on top of the best radical books
we publish?

Then sign up to be the first to hear about our
new books, as well as special events,
podcasts and videos.

You'll also get 50% off your first order with us
when you sign up.

Come and join us!

Go to bit.ly/PlutoNewsletter